MOROCCO
in Pictures

Francesca Davis Di Piazza

Twenty-First Century Books

Contents

Website address: www.lernerbooks.com

Twenty-First Century Books
A division of Lerner Publishing Group
241 First Avenue North
Minneapolis, MN 55401 U.S.A.

web enhanced @ www.vgsbooks.com

Library of Congress Cataloging-in-Publication Data

DiPiazza, Francesca Davis.
    Morocco in pictures / Francesca Davis DiPiazza.
      p. cm. − (Visual geography series)
    Includes bibliographical references and index.
    ISBN-13: 978-0-8225-2672-8 (lib. bdg. : alk. paper)
    ISBN-10: 0-8225-2672-7 (lib. bdg. : alk. paper)
    1. Morocco−Pictorial works. I. Title. II. Visual geography series (Minneapolis, Minn.)
DT305.2.D56 2007
964.0022'2−dc22   2005037102

Manufactured in the United States of America
1 2 3 4 5 6 − BP − 11 10 09 08 07

INTRODUCTION

Raz el Hanout is an exotic blend of twenty-four spices used in Moroccan cuisine. Every corner spice-grinder in Morocco has a unique version, blending their own combination of spices. Similarly, modern Morocco is a unique mix of influences. Located on the northwestern edge of the African continent, the nation is between the Arab world to the east, the African interior to the south, and Europe to the north. Over the centuries, Morocco has absorbed and blended Berber, Arab, European, and African cultures. Moroccan identity can be as intriguing as Raz el Hanout, with its unexpected mingling of ginger, pepper, and rose petals.

Historically, Morocco was a small part of the North African expanse called the Maghreb—an Arabic word meaning "the land where the sun sets." The Maghreb includes present-day Morocco, Algeria, Tunisia, and northwestern Libya. Morocco remained independent for centuries, protected by natural boundaries. The immense Sahara, a desert as large as the United States, penetrates southern Morocco and stretches across Africa. Its scorching landscape separates

Morocco from the African nations south of the Sahara. The rugged Atlas Mountains run almost the entire length of Morocco. They have protected Morocco from invaders from the east. The Mediterranean Sea borders Morocco's northern coast, and the Atlantic Ocean forms its western coast. The European nation of Spain lies just a few miles across the Strait of Gibraltar, the narrow channel linking the Atlantic Ocean and the Mediterranean Sea.

A mountain-dwelling people known as the Berbers have maintained their traditional lifestyle in Morocco's Atlas peaks for four thousand years. Arabs, who first migrated to the Maghreb in the seventh century, are the only outside group to take firm root on Moroccan soil. Morocco was a French protectorate from 1912 to 1956, until Moroccans regained independent rule. French culture and language still influences Moroccans. The large majority of Moroccans consider themselves part of the Arab world, however. They are unified by a shared language, Arabic, and by one religion, Islam.

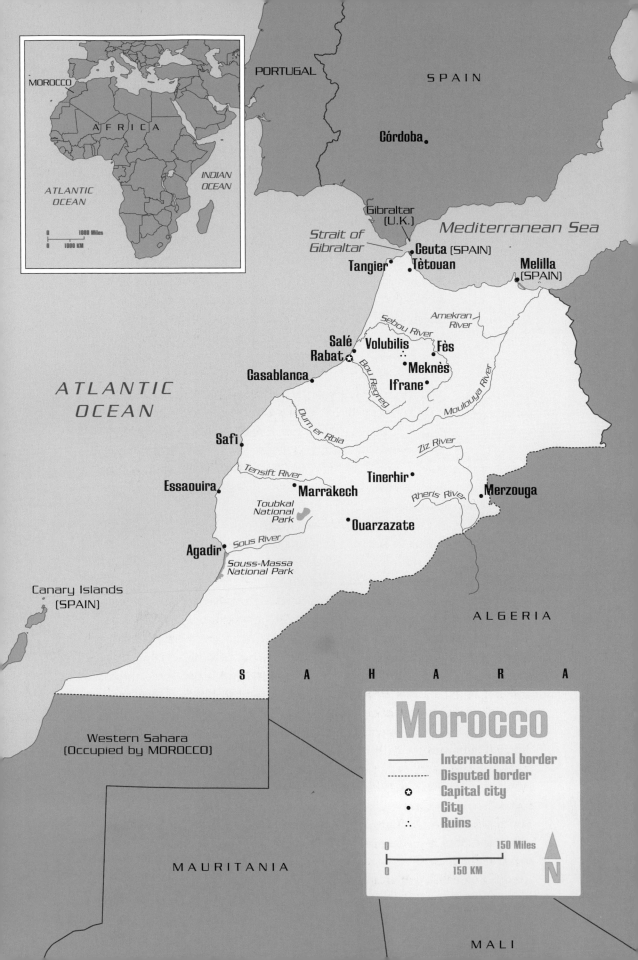

Since Morocco won its independence in 1956, it has seen both impressive technological development and serious social problems. The nation's communication and transportation networks are among the most advanced in North Africa. Yet overpopulation, poverty, drought, and large migrations from poor rural areas to crowded cities are still pressing issues.

In addition to these internal troubles, Morocco's relations with the Western Sahara, which lies to the southwest, are still unsettled. A desert land with an estimated population of 260,000, Western Sahara holds valuable mineral resources. Morocco long claimed the region, based on nine-hundred-year-old boundaries. A small but effective military force called the Polisario opposed Morocco's claim, fighting a war for independence. The neighboring country of Algeria supported the cause of the Polisario, causing poor relations and a border dispute with Morocco.

As a show of good will, Morocco proposed a cease-fire in Western Sahara in 1985, and United Nations (UN) troops were invited to ensure peace until a public vote could be held to decide the future of the territory. More than twenty years later, the vote still has not taken place.

King Muhammad VI became Morocco's ruler and spiritual leader of its huge majority of Muslims (followers of the Islamic religion) following the death of his father, King Hassan II, in 1999. He is modernizing Morocco by encouraging economic and democratic reforms and by promoting the equal rights of women.

But Muslim fundamentalists—whose goal is to have the government function under Sharia, or Islamic law—do not approve of Muhammad VI's rule. Among other things, they disapprove of his alliance with Western nations, whom they view as immoral and corrupt. Fundamentalist influence in Morocco has grown stronger since the success of the 1979 Islamic Revolution in Iran. Most Muslims support the king, but fundamentalists who advocate violence seek to destabilize the government. In 2003 Islamic militants launched suicide bomb attacks in the city of Casablanca. More than forty people were killed. The authorities arrested hundreds of people under antiterrorist laws. The large numbers of poor, uneducated, and unemployed young people are vulnerable to recruitment by fundamentalists. Morocco and the Spanish cities on its Mediterranean coast also serve as illegal gateways to Europe for many poor Africans looking for work. In late 2005, hundreds of sub-Saharan Africans tore through fences surrounding the Spanish enclave Ceuta. Five died, bringing international attention to the plight of people living in extreme poverty.Morocco desperately needs far-reaching education and decent standards of living. The government is devoting considerable resources to improving Morocco's education, health, and employment toward that end.

THE LAND

The Kingdom of Morocco lies in the northwestern corner of the African continent. The nation covers 172,413 square miles (446,550 square kilometers), an area slightly larger than California. Morocco has roughly 1,140 miles (1,835 km) of shoreline. The northern coast runs west along the Mediterranean Sea to the narrow Strait of Gibraltar. Two Spanish enclaves interrupt Morocco's northern coast, the port cities of Ceuta and Melilla. These enclaves are Spanish territory within Moroccan territory. Spain is across the strait, only 9 miles (14 km) to the north. Turning south, Morocco's coast faces the Atlantic Ocean along the entire western border. The Canary Islands, part of Spain, lie in the Atlantic off Morocco's extreme southern coast. Along the southern border lies the Western Sahara (formerly the Spanish Sahara), a desert region that Morocco claims and occupies. Most countries, however, do not recognize Morocco's claim. Algeria borders Morocco on the southeast and east.

▶ **Topography**

High, rugged mountain ranges dominate Morocco's topography. These mountains separate Morocco from the rest of the Maghreb to the east. They also divide the country into four major regions. The Coastal Lowlands region, to the west of the mountains, supports most of the country's population and agriculture. The mountains themselves form the Interior Mountains region. This region includes fertile valleys wedged among the peaks. The northern mountains are geologically unstable, and Morocco is subject to severe earthquakes. The dry, hot Pre-Sahara region is east and south of the mountain ranges, where the High Plateaus region fades into the Sahara Desert.

▶ **Coastal Lowlands**

Bounded on the south and east by the Grand Atlas Mountains, Morocco's Atlantic and Mediterranean coastal strip is flat and regular. Sand dunes or marshes occasionally interrupt this wide, fertile plain.

Two major plains—the Rharb in the north and Doukkala to the southwest—have the richest soil in the country. The majority of Morocco's population is in the western part of the lowland region between the cities of Tangier and Essaouira. The important cities of Rabat and Casablanca are on the Atlantic coast as well.

The Coastal Lowlands rise to a broad plateau toward the east, at the foothills of the mountains. This barren plateau is rich in the valuable phosphate rock from which it takes its name—the Phosphates Plateau. Two farmable plains—the Tadla and the Haouz—lie between the phosphates plateau and the mountains. The rivers flowing out of the Atlas ranges provide these areas with water.

Interior Mountains

Three sections of the Atlas Mountains form the major barrier between the Atlantic Ocean and the Sahara. The Middle Atlas Mountains in the northeast include peaks that rise from 4,000 to 10,000 feet (1,219 to 3,048 meters) above sea level. In ancient times, the only access from east to west in the area was through the narrow Taza Gap, an opening between the Er Rif and Middle Atlas ranges.

Er Rif is a group of mountains in the north that runs parallel to the Mediterranean coast. These mountains seldom reach more than 7,000 feet (2,134 m) above sea level. The range drops steeply into the Mediterranean Sea and cuts off most of the country from the northern Tangier Peninsula. Er Rif is the heartland of the Berber people.

Tinerhir village lies in the **Middle Atlas Mountains** near two oases.

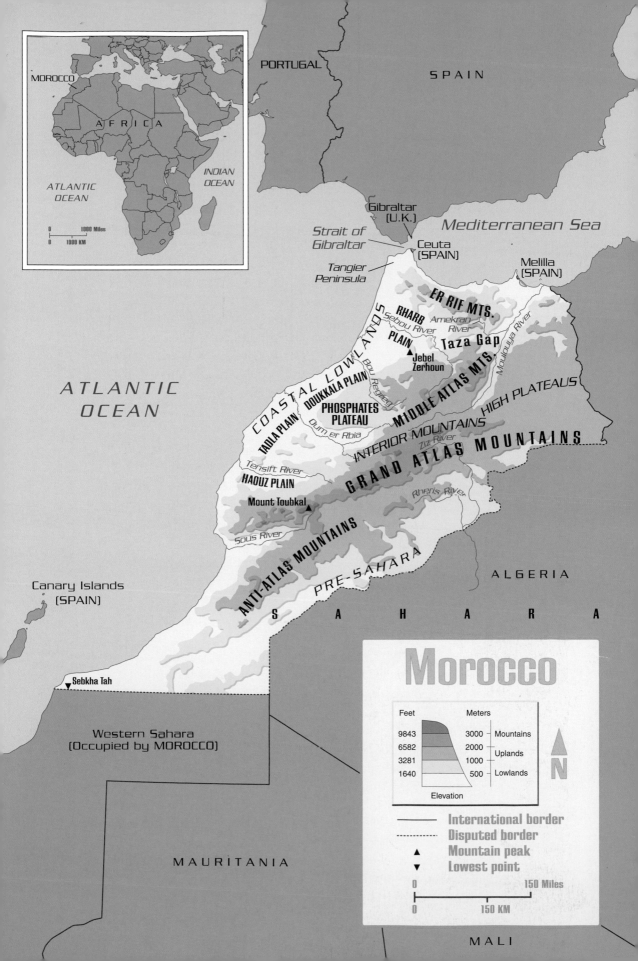

MOROCCO

AFRICA

ATLANTIC
OCEAN

INDIAN
OCEAN

0   1000 Miles
0   1000 KM

PORTUGAL

SPAIN

Gibraltar
(U.K.)

Strait of
Gibraltar

Tangier
Peninsula

Ceuta
[SPAIN]

Mediterranean Sea

Melilla
[SPAIN]

ER RIF MTS.

RHARB
Sebou River   Amekran
River

PLAIN   Taza Gap

Jebel
Zerhoun

MIDDLE ATLAS MTS.

HIGH PLATEAUS

Moulouya River

ATLANTIC
OCEAN

COASTAL LOWLANDS

DOUKKALA PLAIN

PHOSPHATES
PLATEAU

TADLA PLAIN

Oum er Rbia

Bou Regreg

INTERIOR MOUNTAINS

Ziz River

GRAND ATLAS MOUNTAINS

Tensift River

HAOUZ PLAIN

Rheris River

Mount Toubkal ▲

Sous River

ANTI-ATLAS MOUNTAINS

PRE-SAHARA

S A H A R A

ALGERIA

Canary Islands
[SPAIN]

▼ Sebkha Tah

Western Sahara
(Occupied by MOROCCO)

MAURITANIA

Morocco

Feet	Meters	
9843	3000	Mountains
6582	2000	Uplands
3281	1000	
1640	500	Lowlands

Elevation

N

——— International border
- - - - Disputed border
▲ Mountain peak
▼ Lowest point

0   150 Miles
0   150 KM

MALI

The second and third sections of the Atlas Mountains—the Grand Atlas Mountains in the central part of the region and the Anti-Atlas Mountains in the south—are tall and wide enough to produce a nationwide split in climate. Their peaks prevent moist coastal winds from meeting the dry winds off the Sahara. The mountains are snowcapped in winter and burnt dry red in summer. The main stretch of the Grand Atlas Mountains has summits over 10,000 feet (3,048 m), and ski resorts are located here. The most impressive peak is Mount Toubkal (13,665 ft. or 4,165 m), the highest mountain in North Africa.

◐ The High-Plateaus and the Pre-Sahara

East of the Middle Atlas Mountains is the High Plateaus region. These elevated flatlands make up a level region about 3,500 feet (1,067 m) above the sea. These plateaus, combined with the Taza Gap farther north, form an important communications and transportation route between Morocco and neighboring Algeria.

South of the High Plateaus and to the east of the Anti-Atlas range lies the Pre-Sahara region. This region is composed of *hamaidiya*—sun-baked, rocky wasteland. Berber people live in oasis settlements here, where underground water comes close to the surface. They raise fruit, dates, and olive trees. Here begins the small portion of the Sahara Desert enclosed within Morocco's official boundaries. The spectacular sand dunes of the settlement of Merzouga are some of the highest—and most photographed—dunes in the world.

◐ Rivers

Morocco's river system is the biggest in North Africa, but none of the rivers are navigable. Many dams harness the rivers' rushing water to create hydroelectric power. The dams also collect water for crop irrigation.

Rivers in Morocco generally flow northwest to the Atlantic Ocean and southeast to the Sahara. The chief exception is the Moulouya River, which empties into the Mediterranean Sea. Five major rivers—the Sebou, Bou Regreg, Oum er Rbia, Tensift, and Sous—empty into the Atlantic. The Sebou and its tributaries provide 45 percent of the country's water resources. The Ziz and the Rheris are the two major waterways running into the Sahara. These streams lose much of their force through evaporation and eventually dry up completely in the desert heat.

▶ Climate

Morocco shares its latitude with the major deserts of the world. The country's weather is dominated by an almost permanent high-pressure system, which brings sunny weather. Interior mountains divide the country into two climatic regions. In northern and central Morocco, moderate weather prevails. Winters there are cool and wet, with plentiful rainfall. Summers in these areas are dry and hot—despite brisk sea breezes in the afternoon. Moving inland, south and east, hot conditions are common. The desert climate brings little rain, hot summers, and mild winters.

Rabat, Morocco's capital city, has pleasant temperatures averaging 63°F (17°C) in winter and 77°F (25°C) in summer. Marrakech has average temperatures of 66°F (19°C) in winter and 91°F (33°C) in summer. In the Grand Atlas Mountains, temperatures fall below freezing in the winter, and summers are cool and pleasant, with occasional thunderstorms.

Morocco's eastern border meets the Sahara Desert. The climate there is hot and dry. To see more pictures of Morocco, visit www.vgsbooks.com for links.

Moving south from the Mediterranean coast, rainfall in Morocco falls from an average of 40 inches (101 centimeters) annually in the Er Rif region to less than 5 inches (13 cm) in the southern desert. The coastal city of Rabat sees an annual average of 21 inches (53 cm) of rain. An average of 9 inches (23 cm) of rain falls every year in the inland city of Marrakech. Serious droughts occasionally strike the country. These periods of insufficient rainfall reduce agricultural harvests and threaten people's livelihoods.

Flora and Fauna

The diverse Moroccan countryside features a wide range of plant life. Groves of olive, almond, and citrus fruit trees—oranges, grapefruits, and lemons—are abundant. When almond trees bloom white in springtime, the hills look as if they are blanketed with snow. The western plateaus are covered with various grasses. Esparto grass is used to make fine paper. Date palms thrive in dry lands, near oases. Dates are an important cash crop and a staple food for people and animals. One palm can yield up to 600 pounds (272 kilograms) of fruit a year. The trees also provide building materials and fiber for rope. Shade from their broad fronds lowers heat and reduces water evaporation. The spiny argan tree grows only in a few places in the world, including Morocco. This hardy, twisted tree, also known as Moroccan ironwood, grows no higher than 20 feet (6 m) tall. Goats climb into its low branches to eat its leaves and

Camels are important in parts of Morocco because they are specially adapted for life in the desert. They are domesticated animals—they do not live in the wild.

leathery fruits. Humans use argan nut oil in cosmetics and cooking.

Forests cover nearly an estimated 15 percent of the county's area. The thickest and most varied growth is found in the Middle Atlas Mountains, where evergreen oaks, pine, cedar, and juniper flourish. Morocco's forests were more abundant before overgrazing and extensive woodcutting led to soil erosion in many areas. In addition, the leather tanning (processing) industry strips vast stands of green and cork oaks of their bark. The bark is also harvested for cork bottle stoppers. Government programs plant imported eucalyptus trees as windbreaks.

People have long inhabited Morocco's plains and coasts, and their domesticated animals have replaced many wild animals. Jackals, rabbits, porcupines, and hedgehogs are still abundant, however. Morocco's highlands are home to wild boars, mountain cats, and Barbary sheep, Africa's only wild sheep. (*Barbary* is a name used in the past for "North Africa.") Lions once roamed the Atlas Mountains, but the last Atlas lion died in captivity in the 1960s. In Er Rif, hunters use ferrets (weasel-like mammals) to catch rabbits. The macaque, or Barbary ape, is North Africa's only monkey. Macaques live in family groups of ten to thirty animals, mostly in the Middle Atlas cedar forests.

The mountains are full of bird life, including hawks, eagles, owls, vultures, and the huge lammergeier, or golden eagle. The kite is a bird that nests in high rocky areas. It sometimes kills prey by knocking small animals off rocks with its powerful wings. Doves and partridges are common throughout the country.

Many desert animals are nocturnal, or active at night when it is cool. Striped hyenas and golden jackals hunt at night in the country's dry eastern sections. The fennec, or desert fox, sleeps in burrows under the hot sand during the day. Predators feed on the many rodents, including

MOROCCO'S MULES

Morocco's mountain dwellers still rely on mules. These sure-footed beasts of burden have been bred in North Africa since about 1750 B.C. With 800,000 mules, Morocco has the second-largest number of mules in Africa. The animals are the offspring of a male donkey (a jack) and a female horse (a mare). The correct term for the offspring of a male horse (a stallion) and a female donkey (a jenny) is a hinny. Hinnies are smaller than mules and less popular. Known for being fast and accurate kickers, mules are stronger than horses and can work for more years. They can tolerate extreme temperatures, survive on a limited diet, and are resistant to illness.

jerboas and sand rats, that live in dry lands. The dry southwestern region is home to the Barbary squirrel, which feeds on argan nuts. Scorpions can endure the hottest deserts and survive on little food or water. These nocturnal animals belong to the same class that spiders do, Arachnida. At least three kinds are found in Morocco, including the African fat-tailed scorpion. Poisonous snakes—such as vipers, puff adders, and cobras—mostly live in the south.

The seacoast is rich in sea life. Porpoises and dolphins frolic around the Strait of Gibraltar. In the south, a few endangered monk seals live off Morocco's Atlantic coast. Fishers catch 240 species of fish along the country's shores. Sardines are the most important fish for the fishing trade. Perch, sole, shrimp, squid, octopus, oysters, and other shellfish also make up the daily catch. Seabirds include gulls, terns, and cormorants. Birds migrating to and from Europe, including greater flamingos from southern France, stop over on the coasts.

Natural Resources and Environmental Concerns

Phosphate rock, a key ingredient in fertilizers, is the natural asset that brings Morocco its greatest export income. Morocco also has large deposits of iron ore, manganese, lead, zinc, and salt. The country's hydroelectric power, coal, natural gas, and petroleum (crude oil) do not fully meet its energy needs. The government is investing in projects to harness the power of two of Morocco's most abundant resources: wind and sun.

Morocco benefits from its location at the close juncture of Africa and Europe, especially in trade and tourism. Many tourists come to see Morocco's beautiful landscapes and fascinating culture, so close to Europe and yet so distinct.

However, Morocco faces some serious environmental challenges, including desertification, or the process of dry land becoming desert. Desertification results from climate stresses, such as drought, and from heavy use of dry lands. Too many people struggling for essentials such as water, food, shelter, and fuel damages the land. Too much livestock grazing strips away plant life.

Morocco is also subject to water scarcity, a problem when a country's population is larger than the available water resources. Morocco struggles with water pollution. Raw sewage and soil runoff contaminate water supplies. Oil spills and the routine flushing of oil tanker tanks pollute coastal waters.

Thirty-four animal species in Morocco are endangered, or threatened with dying out. The Moroccan government is working to protect the country's ecosystem. National parks protect plant and animal habitats. The Toubkal National Park in the Grand Atlas covers 89,000 acres (36,000 hectares). The Souss-Massa National Park protects a region that includes ocean cliffs, sand dunes, and forests. Many rare animals and a wide variety of birds live there. Tree plantation programs are also under way in Morocco, planting millions of trees as windbreaks and green belts in dry regions.

◉ Cities

Morocco has had four capitals in its history: Rabat, Marrakech, Fès, and Meknès. These cities are known as the royal cities. In modern times, Rabat is the nation's capital city, Marrakech is its tourist center, Fès is the country's spiritual heart, and Meknès retains the feel of a traditional Berber town.

Other large cities are also important. Like many other developing countries, Morocco has experienced huge migrations of rural dwellers to its industrialized cities. Drought, poverty, and poor social services such as education drive many peasants and mountain dwellers to leave their traditional lifestyles. The Moroccan government has built huge housing projects, but large slums remain proof of severe shortages of affordable housing and jobs in cities.

Casablanca is Morocco's largest city. In this city view, the famous Hassan II Mosque (Islamic house of worship) is seen in the background.

Visit www.vgsbooks.com for links to websites with additional information about things to see and do in Morocco's cities, local weather, population statistics, and more!

CASABLANCA is the industrial, commercial, and financial hub of Morocco. With a population of almost 3.6 million people, it is Morocco's largest city. Its name means "white house" in Spanish. Casablanca is famous for its whitewashed buildings, which reflect the heat of the sun. Portuguese explorers founded the modern city in the 1500s. Casablanca is a city of extremes. New hotels and businesses stand in sharp contrast to slums. Casablanca does not have enough jobs for all the thousands of uneducated workers in the slums.

RABAT, with about 1.8 million inhabitants, is the modern capital of Morocco. Its name comes from *ribat*, Arabic for a "well-protected holy place." The city, established in the 1200s, became prominent during the French occupation of the 1900s. Rabat's chief business is government. The king's residence, one of the monarchy's grandest palaces, is in this city. The capital city is one of the largest manufacturing centers in the country and is known for its fine textiles and carpets. Many of Rabat's wide streets are lined with palm trees and bright flowering shrubs.

Colorful and carefully designed rugs hang on display in an outdoor market (*souk*) in Rabat.

⊙ Other Cities

With an estimated 1 million people, Marrakech is Morocco's main tourist center, famous for its beautiful gardens and mosques. Called the Red City for the red earth walls that enclose it, Marrakech was a regional marketplace for centuries. A vast network of markets still showcases handmade crafts, street entertainers, and food sellers. The Grand Atlas Mountains form a stunning backdrop to the city.

Fès (population 753,000) is the spiritual and cultural center of the nation. Fès University is one of the best-known institutions in the Islamic world. Beginning in the ninth century A.D., Muslim leaders beautified Fès with mosques. Rich merchants built palaces of white marble, fragrant woods, and green and blue tiles. A red felt, brimless hat called a fez is named after the city.

Berbers first settled on the fertile plains around Mcknès in the 800s. Sultan Moulay Ismail made Meknès his capital in the 1600s. Despite a population of 530,171, Meknès has the feel of a Berber town. Outside the city walls, fruit orchards produce apricots, peaches, and plums. Nearby Jebel Zerhoun is a holy mountain where pilgrims come to visit the tombs of Berber holy men.

Until Morocco achieved independence in 1956, Europeans occupied and governed Tangier. Because of its strategic location on the Strait of Gibraltar, Tangier has long been of political importance. Modern Tangier, with more than 526,000 inhabitants, is a major port, the gateway to Spain, and also a popular tourist resort. Its Mediterranean climate is perfect for fruit trees. Tangerines take their name from the city.

MARRAKECH'S PROTECTIVE PALMS

Date palm groves surround Marrakech, and palm trees line the city's streets. It is illegal to cut down a palm, so they grow in the middle of sidewalks too. The original development plan for the city said that no building is allowed to be higher than a palm tree. Palm trees are important in the desert environment, and they symbolize protection and prosperity. *Ennakhil* is the word for "palm tree" in Arabic, and it is also the name of a charity started in 1997 in Marrakech. This organization works with women and children in the area to increase their standard of living, focusing on education, job training, and health.

HISTORY AND GOVERNMENT

Archaeologists believe that eight thousand years ago, the southern Sahara was a fertile savanna (grassland). The land supported much game and many hunters. Ancient artists left behind evidence of their lives in paintings and carvings on rock walls. They depicted people and the animals around them, including crocodiles, giraffes, and elephants.

Gradual changes in the area's climate turned the savanna into desert. After 4000 B.C., a late Stone Age people continued to live and hunt along the northwestern coast of Africa. Around 2000 B.C., their descendants began to mix with a people who had migrated from southwestern Asia. These immigrants, called the Berbers, were farmers and herders. They established control over the vast Maghreb, including the area that is now Morocco. Over the centuries, Moroccan rock art reflected these changes in local climate, cultures, and animals. Gradually, pictures of domesticated cattle and camels replaced images of wild animals.

Phoenicians and Romans

The Phoenicians were seafaring merchants from present-day Lebanon. They founded the city of Carthage on the coast of present-day Tunisia around the 800s B.C. Phoenician rulers used this city as the cornerstone of their great empire, which included most of the lands of the Maghreb. The Phoenicians often paid Berber leaders to protect their trading caravans, or convoys, into the African interior.

By the first century A.D., the Roman Empire, based in Italy, had conquered Carthage and extended its military power into northern Morocco. The Romans were great builders. They modernized Morocco by improving the ports, irrigating the land, and building roads and fortresses. They also seized most of the best land from the Berbers, dividing it up among Roman settlers. Many Berbers retreated to mountainous regions. From the mountains, they staged frequent attacks on Roman outposts.

The Vandals and the Byzantines

By the fifth century, overtaxation and poor management had greatly weakened the Roman Empire. The Vandals—a northern European people—invaded North Africa in 429. They overran the Maghreb and ruled Morocco for the next century. Berber raids on the new rulers continued as they had during the Roman period. But it was the Byzantine Empire that drove the Vandals from Morocco.

The Byzantine state, or the Eastern Roman Empire, had its capital at Constantinople (present-day Istanbul, Turkey). From there, the emperor Justinian took control of the territories in North Africa and advanced into Morocco. Although he defeated the Vandals, Justinian had little support from the Berbers—or even from his own army, which he paid badly and treated harshly. Berber raiders, taking advantage of Justinian's weak administration, regained the land and held it until Arab armies attacked a century later.

Arab Invasion

A new faith, Islam, arose on the Arabian Peninsula in the early 600s, founded by the prophet (spiritual spokesperson) Muhammad. As part of a highly organized religious expansion, Islamic armies came through the Taza Gap in 683. Arab commander Oqba ben Nafi led his army on a western march through the territory. Legend has it that when he reached the Atlantic coast of Morocco, he rode his horse out into the surf and proclaimed, "O God I take you to witness that there is no ford [bridge] here. If there was I would cross it."

Arab armies took control of the area in 710, when a Muslim Arab force under Musa ben Nasser conquered the coastal Berbers. In the four centuries that followed, Berbers absorbed Arab culture, religion, and language. Mountain Berbers remained free of Arab political control but converted to Islam. The religion created a shared Arab identity among the different peoples of Morocco. Few traces remained of civilizations that had conquered them.

In 711 the governor, Tariq ibn Zayid, led a new army of Berber converts across the Strait of Gibraltar to invade Vandal-held Spain. The successful Arab and Berber soldiers defeated the Vandals and settled in the new land. The Muslim conquerors of Spain were known as Moors. The resulting culture, a blend of Spanish and Moroccan, is called Moorish.

In the late 700s, Arab Moulay (Master) Idris Abdallah united a group of western Berbers known as the Awraba. A sharif, or direct descendant of the prophet Muhammad, Idris established the Awraba as the cornerstone of the first truly Moroccan state. Idris was assassinated in 792, but his son—Moulay Idris II—was able to hold the state

A **merchant caravan** crosses a stream in the Sahara Desert.

together. He also founded the city of Fès in 808. His descendants established borders that are still used to define Morocco's boundaries.

The Idrisids (Idris family) firmly established hereditary rule by sharifs. Religious law bound the dynasty together until Idris II divided his state into equal parts to be ruled by his sons. These smaller kingdoms attacked one another. Mountain Berbers and Muslim armies from Spain also attacked the divided realm. In the tenth century, a Muslim emir (prince) from Córdoba, Spain, captured northern Morocco.

The Beginning of Berber Unity

In the early 1000s, Berbers united for the first time as a political force. Leaders of one union of Berbers—the Sanhaja—accepted a strict Muslim teacher named ibn Yasin as their spiritual head. Ibn

Yasin established a holy place called a ribat. He named his Sanhaja students the Almoravids, meaning "men of the ribat."

In the mid-eleventh century, the Bedouin, a nomadic Arab people from northeastern Africa, migrated to Morocco and to other regions of the Maghreb. For two hundred years, this group converted much of the Berber-held farmland into pasture for their herds.

By the end of the eleventh century, the Almoravids controlled the northwestern quarter of the African continent and part of Spain. (Morocco's current claim to the Western Sahara is based on the boundaries established during Almoravid rule.) The Almoravids took Marrakech as their capital but allowed local leaders to retain power.

By the twelfth century, Almoravid leaders came to accept a looser interpretation of the Quran (Islamic holy writings). The Sanhaja troops, who favored a stricter code, rebelled. Another religious reform group—the Almohads—overpowered the Almoravid dynasty during its struggle with the Sanhaja.

The Moors in Spain

Like the Almoravids, the Almohads controlled part of Spain. Eventually the dynasty moved its base of power from North Africa to Spain. The Almohad scholars and artists in Spain were part of the Arab world's great advances during the Middle Ages. Arab culture gradually filtered into Europe. In 1248 the Moors began building the elaborate Alhambra palace in Granada, Spain. The Alhambra remains one of the most important Islamic structures in the Western

The **Islamic Alhambra palace** is located in Granada, in southern Spain. The palace is lavishly decorated throughout with stone and wood carvings and tile patterns.

world. Arab learning helped foster the Renaissance, a rebirth of the arts in Christian Europe in the coming centuries.

During the thirteenth century, however, the Almohads in Morocco lost power to a third Berber dynasty—the Merinids. After decades of rebellion, the Merinids captured Marrakech in 1271. The last of the Almohads were executed in public outside Marrakech five years later. The Merinids created a new capital, Rabat, on the site of a captured Almohad fortress.

Trade, scholarship, and art flourished under the Merinids. The Merinids were unable, however, to extend the borders of their state as far as the previous unified Berber empires. The Maghreb divided into rival dynasties. These dynasties encouraged scholarship and funded religious schools called *merdesas*. Architecture soared to new heights. The beautiful Attarine Merdesa in Fès was a seat of learning in jewel-like surroundings. Mosaics, marble, and cedarwood created a place of harmony for religious studies.

The 1300s also saw the spread of the Sufi branch of Islam through North Africa. Sufis emphasized personal spiritual practices rather than outward observation of religious laws. They encouraged a charitable and peaceful way of life. However, the fourteenth century saw competing armies clash in continual wars. This strife was matched by constant intrigue among ruling families.

Crusaders and Pirates

A renewal of Christian European power ended Merinid rule. Christian armies embarked on Crusades, or religious wars. The crusaders' ultimate aim was to regain the holy city of Jerusalem (in present-day Israel) from Muslim control. Though this didn't happen, Christian armies of northern Spain did win southern Spain from the Muslims. In 1492 the Spanish Christians defeated the last of the Moorish kingdoms in Spain. The seven-hundred-year-old culture of Moorish Spain was swept aside by Christian fundamentalists and Spanish Jews were expelled from their country.

During the 1500s, Muslim North Africa battled on land and sea with Christian crusaders from Spain and Portugal. Spanish Christian armies invaded Morocco and established military outposts at Ceuta and Melilla. But the riches of the newly discovered Americas were of more immediate interest to the Spanish.

Portugal was more of a threat to Moroccan independence than Spain. Portugal was a trading power and wanted to control access to the seas. The Portuguese seized strategic ports on the northern coasts of Morocco and thus controlled the Strait of Gibraltar—and access to the Mediterranean Sea. Starting in 1505, they also expanded south along the Atlantic coast, establishing their military presence in captured harbor towns as far south as Agadir.

European forces captured and lost North African Mediterranean ports many times. North African pirates such as the great Algerian-based Khayr al-Din, known as Barbarossa (Redbeard), battled with Christian fleets for control of the Mediterranean sea-lanes. No European force, however, permanently controlled the interior of Morocco.

The growing Ottoman Empire meanwhile extended its influence from its center in modern-day Turkey. Ottoman power spread across southwestern Asia and most of North Africa. Morocco was the only Maghreb region that did not fall under the control of this superpower in the 1500s.

The Saadians and the Alawis

Although peoples in some parts of the Maghreb accepted a strict form of Islam, many in the interior followed the teachings of Sufi marabouts, or wandering holy men. Marabouts were especially popular among isolated Berber groups. In 1510 the marabouts selected an Arab group with blood ties to Muhammad—the Saadians—to lead a jihad, or holy struggle, against the Christian Europeans in Morocco.

The most effective Saadi leader was Ahmed al-Mansur, who came to power in 1578. His soldiers reclaimed Ceuta, among other strategic points. Al-Mansur adopted administrative methods from the Ottoman Turks to govern his newly captured territory. Pashas, or governors, ruled each area. A caid, or tax collector, supported the pasha with enough military strength to police the area. The leader of this ruling dynasty came to be called a sultan, who enjoyed absolute power. The dynasty collected taxes from a population estimated to be between 3 and 7 million people. Money also came from taxes on the trans-Saharan trade.

In 1594 Ahmed al-Mansur received his first wealth from his trans-Saharan expedition: thirty mules loaded with gold. *Al-Mansur* means "the victorious." Soon Ahmed was also known as *al-Dahhabi*, "the golden."

In 1591 al-Mansur sent an expedition across the Sahara to capture people for his slave trade. Members of the expedition established forts at desert positions and took control of the great trading city Timbuktu (in present-day Mali). These outposts enabled al-Mansur to transport slaves from the interior of Africa across the desert. During al-Mansur's reign, Morocco became one of the continent's leading centers of trade in spices, cloth, and ivory.

After al-Mansur died in 1603, weak successors could not prevent pashas and marabouts from rebelling, and disorder increased. Of the next twelve Saadi sultans who ruled, eight were assassinated. The Alawis, who had migrated from Arabia during the Merinid dynasty, rose in power. They fought the marabouts in another jihad. Like the earlier followers of Idris, the Alawis believed in rule by sharifs, Muhammad's descendants.

In 1610 Morocco saw another influx of immigrants. That year King Philip III of Spain expelled all Spaniards of Muslim descent from the country. About 300,000 refugees fled to Morocco. Many settled near Rabat, where some engaged in piracy against European ships.

Moulay Ismail and His Successors

By 1663 competing factions had driven Morocco into civil war. In the midst of the chaos, a leader arose from the Alowite family. The Alowites were sharifs who had moved to Morocco from Arabia in the 1200s. In 1664 the young warrior, Moulay Rashid, became the first Alowite sultan. A brilliant military leader, he quickly achieved full control of Morocco with his Bedouin army. But he died in a nighttime riding accident in the palace gardens of Marrakech in 1672.

Moulay Ismail succeeded his brother and reigned as the Alowite sultan for fifty-five years. His descendants still rule Morocco. Ismail organized the kingdom so successfully that the Ottoman Turks remained unable to gain control of Morocco. Ismail also forced out remaining Christian posts on the Atlantic coast. The sultan did see value in European contacts, however, and exchanged diplomats with France. This decision marked the beginning of French influence in Morocco. Ismail, a strong leader, also had a reputation for cruelty. Thousands of slaves were worked to death in his gigantic building schemes. He had thirty palaces built, as well as bridges and roads. Fond of animals, he kept forty well-fed cats in his palace. He died in 1727, having elevated Morocco to a wealthy and unified power. He also had hundreds of children but no clear successor.

The title *moulay* means "master" in Arabic. However, in Islam there is only one Master—Muhammad, the prophet and founder of Islam. Therefore, if a Moroccan prince or leader is named Muhammad, he is instead addressed as Sidi, meaning "My Lord."

Rival factions gained and lost power over the next two decades. Rulers who succeeded Ismail commanded only small, ineffective armies. Although the Alawis remained in power, their territory shrank.

In 1750 Sultan Sidi (Lord) Muhammed restored unity among local groups by renewing the fight against outsiders. He and his forces fought against remaining Christian control of Moroccan cities. He was victorious in removing the Portuguese from their last holdings in Morocco.

During the late-1700s, France and Great Britain grew in power as the Industrial Revolution (the rise of power-driven machinery) strengthened their economies and military forces. Sidi Muhammed negotiated business treaties with these and other trading nations. In 1786 this included the new nation of the United States. By the 1800s, both Spain and France had made investments in Morocco. French manufacturers operated in Morocco's larger cities, and Spain had forts in the Ceuta area.

▶ The Great Game

In 1856 the opening of the Suez Canal in Egypt allowed ships to sail from the Atlantic Ocean through the Mediterranean Sea and on toward the Indian Ocean. As European merchants developed trade in Asia, control of the Strait of Gibraltar and the Mediterranean again became important. Europeans therefore competed to gain power in the Mediterranean regions of North Africa. They sometimes referred to this competition as the "great game."

The Ottoman Empire had weakened by then, leaving no strong leader or political unity in the Maghreb to resist European colonization. The Moroccan sultan, Moulay Hassan (ruled 1873–1894), retained his authority, however. He tried to modernize Morocco and keep it independent.

Looking for natural resources to fuel their growing industries, European interests spread beyond the coasts of North Africa. By the end of the 1800s, the "scramble for Africa" was well under way, as each major European power claimed vast sections of the African continent. France insisted on ruling Morocco as well as its enormous holdings in French West Africa. Spain, however, continued to claim a part of the country.

By 1900 more than ten thousand European settlers lived in Morocco. Sultan Abdul Aziz had neither the military strength nor the regional unity needed to resist the Europeans. In 1907 the entrance of the French army into Casablanca marked the end of Moroccan independence. Morocco was one of the last African states to come under foreign control.

The sultan's brother, Moulay Hafid, ousted Abdul Aziz in 1908, but it was too late to stop French expansion in Morocco. In 1912 Hafid signed the Treaty of Fès. It made Morocco a French protectorate, or dependent state. Later in the year, the Spanish signed a similar document, gaining control over the previously French-dominated northern coast and the Rif. To make sure that the Strait of Gibraltar would remain open, European powers made Tangier into an international zone under their shared rule.

Early Colonial Rule

The first French resident-general in Morocco was Louis-Hubert-Gonzalve Lyautey. Lyautey believed that the French should strengthen the sultan's central government and its control over the various Berber groups in the mountain regions. This policy, he felt, would eventually allow the French to leave Morocco in the hands of a local Islamic government that was both secure and pro-French.

Under Lyautey, France built schools, hospitals, bridges, and other improvements in Morocco. The colonial government trained Moroccans for official posts in the French-run administration. Within two years, the resident-general had unified the region of central Morocco, from Fès to Marrakech. World War I (1914–1918), however, temporarily halted French conquest.

In 1921 the Spanish colonial forces in northern Morocco tried to subdue the Berbers of Er Rif. The Berbers joined together under Abd al-Krim, a skilled military leader. Al-Krim established the Rif Republic, an independent state governed by Moroccan Berbers and Arabs. In 1924 al-Krim's 120,000-man army pushed into French

Morocco, fighting right up to Fès. The French and Spanish joined forces to crush the rebellion in 1926. Though destroyed, the Rif Republic became a symbol of the Moroccan people's desire for independence.

The Rise of Nationalism

Thousands of French settlers, called colons, moved into Morocco during the early 1900s. Through pressure from the colons, French policy changed from one of aiding the Moroccan government to one of weakening it. The French educational system—which did not teach Arabic or Islam—was introduced for Moroccan children. Colonial officials began to support selected pashas and marabouts, hoping to weaken the sultan's authority.

Nationalist (patriotic) groups formed to resist French authority. The most important one was made up of Moroccan students from French-run schools. They formed the Istiqlal (Freedom) Party and pressed for national independence.

The nationalist cause was greatly helped by Muhammad V, whom the French had appointed as sultan in 1927. The French intended the sultan, who was only seventeen years old, to be a defender of their colonial policies. In public speeches, however, Muhammad V referred to the rights of the Moroccan people and to their long history of independence prior to French rule.

In addition to speaking on nationalist topics, the sultan signed the Plan of Reforms submitted to him in 1934 by nationalist leaders. This move angered the French but gained Muhammad V support throughout the nation. Anti-French demonstrations and riots occurred frequently in Morocco in the 1930s.

Independence

During World War II (1939–1945), Morocco resisted the Axis (pro-German) forces and served as a base for Britain and the United States. Muhammad V hoped that the Allies (anti-German nations) would support Moroccan independence after the war. This hope was

Franklin Roosevelt *(left)* and Winston Churchill *(right)* confer during the Casablanca Conference in 1943.

strengthened when Morocco's leader met with Britain's prime minister Winston Churchill and U.S. president Franklin Roosevelt at the Casablanca Conference in 1943. The conference laid plans to drive the Axis from Mediterranean regions.

World War II ended in an Allied victory, but its enormous cost in money and lives weakened European colonial powers. Independence movements across Africa gained strength after the war. The French tried to stop Muhammad V's nationalistic efforts by forcing him to sign royal orders limiting the sultan's power. The sultan refused to sign anything that would weaken either the nationalist movement or his own position.

The French eventually replaced the sultan with one of his relatives who was easier to control. In 1953 Muhammad V and his family were exiled to the island of Madagascar off the coast of southeastern Africa. Moroccan reaction was strong. Violence and rioting broke out in the nation.

Spurred by this national reaction, the membership of the Istiqlal Party grew to eighty thousand in the early 1950s. The Army of National Liberation grew out of this membership and turned to violent action. During the two years of the sultan's exile, members of the army killed several hundred French settlers.

To quiet the situation, the French returned Muhammad V to Morocco in 1955. On November 6 of that year, France agreed to end their rule and to recognize Morocco as an independent nation. On March 2, 1956, Muhammad V and his new government began their administration of independent Morocco.

Early Moroccan Policy

Muhammad V enjoyed great popular support, both as a royal figure and as a hero of the independence movement. Because of this popularity, the sultan was able to rule without a written constitution. In 1957 Muhammad V gave himself the European title of king. He appointed his son, Moulay Hassan, crown prince, or successor to the throne.

In 1958 Morocco joined the Arab League—a group of Arab states dedicated to Arab unity. But Muhammad V made an effort to preserve Morocco's neutral international position. For example, Morocco accepted aid from both the United States and its enemy the Soviet Union (a union of republics including Russia).

The king badly damaged relations with Morocco's neighbors, however, with his claims to a "Greater Morocco." Muhammad V, along with many of his subjects, felt that Morocco was entitled to the former Spanish colony of the Western Sahara—and to territories in present-day Mauritania and Mali—because of boundaries established centuries earlier. The French had never clearly divided their holdings in Morocco and Algeria, and both countries claimed territory along the unclear border.

Soon this issue threatened to separate Morocco from both the African and Arab worlds. Consequently, Muhammad V gave up his claims to all of the disputed regions except the Western Sahara. Morocco was then invited in 1961 to join the newly formed Organization of African Unity (OAU), a group of moderate African states.

King Hassan II

One month after the first OAU conference, Muhammad V died after surgery. His son assumed the throne as King Hassan II. The new king reassured Moroccans that he would carry out the policies of his father.

In 1962 Hassan II drafted Morocco's first constitution, which the Moroccan people overwhelmingly approved. The document safeguarded his royal powers and created a legislature, or lawmaking body. But the new constitution failed to produce a stable government. Istiqlal Party members demanded limitations on the king's powers. The legislature voted down laws and reforms that the king drafted.

In 1965 student protests in Casablanca resulted in frequent riots. Demonstrators protested a new law requiring all students to take technical training. Police and army forces killed more than four hundred people. Hassan II blamed the Casablanca riots on the legal system. He therefore declared a state of emergency and took control of the government.

In 1970 the king submitted another constitution, increasing the king's powers, and 98 percent of Moroccan voters approved it. After the selection of the new one-house legislature, Hassan II finally ended the state of emergency.

Between 1971 and 1972, two attempted coups (sudden overthrows of government) occurred. Important government and military officials plotted both coups. In response, Hassan II again took control of the government. He assumed charge of the armed forces and tightened national security. Hundreds of suspects were put in prison without trial, including the young children of General Oufkir, one of the 1972 coup plotters. A third constitution was passed that year, but no elections for a legislature were held.

Hassan II turned his attention again to the Western Sahara, which he still hoped to claim for Morocco. After Spain withdrew its forces from the disputed territory in 1975, Hassan II organized the Green March. (Green is the traditional color of Islam.) This event brought together 350,000 Moroccans who marched into the Western Sahara carrying Moroccan flags and Qurans.

Soon the Polisario resisted Moroccan control and fought for self-rule in the Western Sahara. Eventually, Morocco committed over 75

Moroccans carrying flags, Qurans, and photos of Hassan II start off on the Green March to claim the Western Sahara on November 6, 1975.

percent of its weaponry and troops to fighting this Algerian-backed military force as the dispute dragged on for years.

Hard Times

Meanwhile, Morocco's economy faced hard times. The struggle against the Polisario was expensive. A drought ruined harvests across the countryside. In the early 1980s, unemployment reached 10 percent overall, with a much higher rate in rural areas.

By the end of the 1980s, the United Nations moved in to monitor a cease-fire and to settle the dispute in Western Sahara. A public vote to decide whether Western Sahara would become a part of Morocco was planned. It was postponed over and over, however, due to disagreements over who was eligible to vote. The future of the territory remained undecided. About 260,000 people live in Western Sahara.

In the early 1990s, Morocco was hit hard again by another drought. As agricultural production fell, unemployment and prices rose and the government had to import grain to feed its people.

The king saw a new threat to his control in the 1990s, as fundamentalist Muslims who want Islam to be the law of the land gained influence. The king comes from a royal family that claims descent from the founder of Islam, the prophet Muhammad. The king's authority as ruler and religious leader has kept many Muslims from challenging his rule. One of the king's titles is Commander of the Faithful. Fundamentalists, however, do not accept that anyone is Commander of the Faithful except Allah (Arabic for "God"). Fundamentalism appeals to some people as a cure for corruption, poverty, and despair. It preaches an ideal of a pure Islam free of Western influence, which many see as immoral and materialistic.

In a move to encourage democracy, changes to the constitution in 1996 created a bicameral (two-house) legislature. The 1997 elections were Morocco's first for a lower house of legislature. More than three thousand candidates ran for 325 seats. The king kept most political control, with the power to appoint and fire top ministers who run the country.

A New King, a New Century

Hassan II died in 1999, after thirty-eight years as king. His son, almost thirty-six years old, succeeded him as King Muhammad VI. The new king quickly demonstrated that he was a strong supporter of social and economic reforms. For years international human rights groups had accused Hassan's government of human rights abuses against its citizens. Spying, illegal arrests, and torture had made many Moroccans afraid to criticize their government. Muhammad replaced the most repressive men who had worked for his father. Under the new king's orders, ten thousand political prisoners were released and notorious hidden prisons were closed. Moderate Islamist parties were allowed to operate legally, and the press was given more freedom of expression. Economic improvements attracted new foreign investors to the country. These changes made Muhammad very popular with Moroccans as they entered the twenty-first century.

Unfortunately, the century soon saw a new threat. On September 11, 2001, terrorist attacks on the United States left nearly three thousand dead. The terrorists had links to the fundamentalist Islamic network al-Qaeda. Morocco was among the first Arab and Islamic states to declare solidarity with the United States in the global war against terror.

Militant Islam came closer to home for Moroccans the next year. Moroccan authorities arrested a group of Saudi Arabians who were preparing an attack on U.S. and British ships in the Strait of Gibraltar. As Morocco gave aid to Western countries against Islamist violence, Muhammad came under criticism from radical Islamists. Fundamentalists also objected to the king's social reforms, especially those giving more rights to women. They saw these changes as being too Western and threatening their strict interpretation of Islam.

King Muhammad VI married Princess Lalla Salma in 2002. Public celebrations for the marriage broke a Moroccan tradition of keeping royal wives hidden.

Morocco was rocked by suicide bombings on May 16, 2003. A series of bombings aimed at Western targets in Casablanca killed more than forty people and wounded many more, mostly Moroccans. Authorities believed that the bombers were linked to al-Qaeda. After the attacks, more than one million Moroccans demonstrated against such violence. Moroccan courts sentenced four local Moroccans to death and eighty-three others to various terms in prison. The government enacted new antiterrorism laws and increased its activities against extremist groups.

One year later, a number of Moroccans were suspects in similar bomb attacks in Madrid, Spain, that killed 191 people. That same year, a powerful earthquake in northern Morocco killed more than 500 people. On a more hopeful note, 2004 saw a new family law granting Moroccan women more equal rights with men. That year the United States declared Morocco a major ally, sharing interests in countering terrorism and supporting U.S. efforts to create a democratic government in Iraq. U.S. aid to Morocco for economic growth and job development for 2004 through 2008 is pledged to be $99 million. The United States also enacted a free trade agreement with Morocco, the first such agreement in Africa. This agreement removes tariffs (taxes) from trade goods, an important economic boost for Morocco.

A visit to Morocco by King Juan Carlos of Spain in 2005 signaled improving relations between those two countries. Facing a common threat of Islamic militants brings the two countries into closer cooperation.

◉ Government

The Kingdom of Morocco is a constitutional monarchy, with a king as head of state. Morocco's constitution of 1972 places much of the nation's administration in the hands of an elected government. All citizens

LOOKING FOR A WAY OUT

The contested issue of Spain's fortified enclaves on Morocco's coast flared in late 2005. Hundreds of sub-Saharan Africans desperate to escape extreme poverty tore through 10-foot-tall (3 m) high-security, razor-wire fences surrounding Ceuta. Five died during the rush and the resulting fight with border police. The immigrants see entering the Spanish city as a way to gain a foothold in Europe. Immigrants seeking to reach Europe also cross from Morocco to Spain in boats. Most are caught and sent back, but hundreds die in the dangerous crossing. Morocco would like Spain to give up its enclaves, but Spain, which has held them for centuries, refuses.

eighteen years or older have the right to vote. Because political parties are allowed, the government is not an absolute monarchy. But the country is not a democracy since the king holds far more power than the legislative or judicial branches. He commands the armed forces and major agencies of the government. And his orders have the force of law.

The king heads Morocco's executive branch. As head of state, the king appoints a prime minister with whom he shares the power to write laws. The king also appoints a cabinet, or board of advisers, to help run the government.

People elect members to the Chamber of Representatives, for five-year terms. Of the 325 members of this lower house, 30 are chosen from a national list of women to ensure a percentage of women representatives. Members of the upper house, the Chamber of Counselors, are chosen by representatives of local council, professional, and labor groups to serve nine years.

Morocco's judicial branch is technically independent, but the king heavily influences it. He presides over the Supreme Council of the Judiciary. This council appoints judges to the Supreme Court and supervises Morocco's courts. Lower courts include regional, appeal, and conciliation courts. The national legal system is based on Islamic and Judaic codes and on traditional Berber law. Local leaders operate Islamic courts in their communities.

Visit www.vgsbooks.com for links to websites with up-to-date information about Morocco's history and government and up-to-date articles on current events in Morroco.

THE PEOPLE

Arabs and Berbers make up 99 percent of Morocco's 30.7 million people. They are the descendants of the native Berber peoples and the Arabs who invaded Morocco starting in the 600s. The remaining 1 percent are Moroccan Jews and the Haratin, descendants of western African slaves. Moroccan Jews at one time numbered more than 200,000, but most moved to the Jewish state of Israel in the 1950s. An estimated 4,000 Jews live in Morocco in the early twenty-first century.

Like other African nations, Morocco's population is very young—30 percent are under 15 years of age, while only 5 percent are over 65. An average Moroccan woman will marry when she is 20 and have an average of 2.5 children. Though this is not a high birth rate, the large number of young women ensures that Morocco's population will continue to grow rapidly. The government views the birth rate as too high, as it already struggles to meet the needs of its citizens. The projected population for 2050 is an estimated 45.2 million people.

Close to 57 percent of Morocco's population resides in urban centers,

mostly in cities west of the Atlas Mountains. The nation's overall population density is 178 people per square mile (69 per sq. km). This is three times denser than North Africa's average. It is about average for a Middle Eastern country and is about one-third lower than Spain's population density.

Berbers

The term *Berber* has long been applied to groups who dominate the mountainous regions of the Maghreb. From the seventh century onward, Arab populations mixed extensively with Berber societies. Thus, most Berbers have adopted Morocco's dominant Arab culture. However, the mountain regions of Morocco are still home to people who converse in a distinct Berber language and maintain their traditional ways of life.

Berber society is based on regional groups formed by family ties. The many distinct Berber societies can be divided geographically

A **Berber woman** sells radishes at an outdoor market in a small coastal town. To learn more about the people of Morocco, visit www.vgsbooks.com for links.

into three major groupings. The Rifians occupy the north, the Berber live in the center of the country and in the Sahara, and the Shluh inhabit the Middle Atlas and the Grand Atlas mountains. Berbers in the mountains lead a harsh life as farmers, as they have for thousands of years. Their isolation cuts them off from easy access to health care and education. But it has allowed them to preserve their language and cultural identity.

Berber comes from the Latin word *barbarus*, which means "barbarian." The Romans used the term for anyone who did not speak their Latin language. Later, the Arabs applied it to people who didn't speak Arabic. The Berbers call themselves Amazigh, or the "Free People."

In modern times, the Moroccan government has tried to unify the country by imposing Arab institutions on the entire population. This has sometimes led to resentment. Berber spokespeople point out that government policy favors Arabs in the competition for employment or advancement. Berbers are proud of their heritage. In Morocco's cities, young Berbers lead a revival of their cultural identity.

Health

Morocco has a good health-care system, though rural areas are underserved. The average Moroccan can expect to live for 70 years (72 years for women and 68 years for men). This life expectancy is average for North Africa but far higher than the life expectancy of 52 years for all

Africans. (An average Spanish person can expect to live for 80 years, one of the highest averages in the world.)

Morocco is a leader in working toward safe childbirth for mothers and babies. The government sponsors intensive training of health-care workers and midwives. Still, less than half of women in childbirth have the aid of skilled medical personnel. An average of 39 Moroccan women die giving birth out of every 10,000 live births. North Africa's average is 45 maternal deaths out of every 10,000 live births. Out of every 1,000 children born in Morocco, 40 die before their first birthday. This is lower than the average for North Africa (49 deaths per 1,000), though dramatically higher than the average of 7 deaths per 1,000 babies in developed countries. Abortion is allowed on physical and mental health grounds or in special cases such as rape.

The government has a national strategy for fighting the spread of HIV/AIDS. The nation's rate of infection is 0.1 percent. Poorer people are eligible for free health care, but the difficulty of reaching remote villages makes such national policies hard to put into action. The government recruits medical workers and doctors for all parts of the country, but health care in rural areas remains severely limited.

Language

Arabic, Morocco's official language, exists in three forms. Classical Arabic is the old, literary language of the Quran. Modern Standard Arabic (MSA) comes from Classical Arabic. MSA is a written language used in the press and in literature across the Arab world. It is also the spoken language of the media—broadcasters on the all-Arab TV station Al Jazeera, for instance, speak MSA. Everyday Arabic, spoken in many different Arab nations, varies widely. Moroccan Arabic, called *darija*, is the dialect (variation) that is the most different from the Arabic dialects of other nations. For example, a Moroccan could only understand a Syrian with difficulty.

Because the government promotes Arabic in Morocco's schools, few educated Moroccans speak Berber dialects. Many Berbers who work in

SPELLING ARABIC

The Arabic alphabet has several sounds that are not used in the English language. This makes exact transliteration (changing one alphabet's letters into another's) impossible. There are many different ways to transliterate Arabic into English. For instance, the name of Islam's prophet and the current king of Morocco can be spelled several different ways in English, including:

Mahomet
Mohammid
Muhammad
Muhammed

cities—as well as Berber schoolchildren—learn Arabic but speak the Berber language when they go back to their homes. Over 50 percent of Berber men speak either Arabic or French. Far fewer Berber women are bilingual, because they often remain in rural villages while their husbands migrate to the cities. Traditional Berber dialects include Rifi in the north, Tamazight in central Morocco, and Tashilhit in the Grand Atlas Mountains.

French is Morocco's unofficial third language. It is the main language of business and is widely used in government and higher education. Spanish is also spoken. Learning English is the growing choice of educated young people.

● Education

Before 1912, schooling for most Moroccans consisted of two or three years of religious training. It emphasized reading and memorizing the Quran. After 1912 the French set up French-style schools, which taught thousands of Moroccans each year. French classes, however, neglected Arab traditions and language. So the Moroccan government has stressed Arab culture in the nation's schools since independence.

Education is a key part of the government's plans to improve citizens' well-being and the country's economic and social growth. Morocco needs skilled, educated workers to keep its economy growing, and the government commits about 22 percent of its spending on education. Education is compulsory for children between the ages of 6 and 13, but only 79 percent of Moroccan children attend school. Many children in remote rural areas do not attend school at all. More boys (84 percent) than girls (74 percent) go to school. The language of instruction is Arabic for the first two years of primary school, then Arabic and French for the next four years, with English as an additional language. Teaching in the Berber language began in primary schools in 2003.

Secondary school lasts for up to six years. Enrollment is only about 38 percent of children aged 13 and up. Again, more boys (43 percent) attend than girls (33 percent). In recent years, the government has given increased attention to girls' education and established several girls' schools, mostly in urban areas.

Almost 300,000 students attend Morocco's fourteen universities. The oldest university in the country is the Islamic University of Fès, founded in 859. The newest is an English-language university founded at Ifrane in 1995. Dozens of vocational schools provide training in business, teaching, agriculture, mining, and other trades.

Morocco's adult literacy rate, or the percentage of adults able to read and write a basic sentence, is 52 percent. The gap between boys and girls attending school is reflected in a very high illiteracy rate for Moroccan women. Almost 60 percent of Moroccan women—more than 6 million people—cannot read and write. Male illiteracy rates are 38 percent, or 3.7 million people. The country addresses its low adult literacy rate through adult education, radio classes, and a newspaper for people just learning to read.

▶ Housing and Sanitation

Economic conditions and lifestyles affect the housing choices of most Moroccans. In the Middle Atlas Mountains and other remote regions, nomadic Arab and Berber families sleep in large tents. When their herds need fresh grazing land, the nomads move with their tents. In the Grand Atlas Mountains, Berber farmers have more permanent dwellings. Their houses are rectangles of sun-dried mud bricks with roofs of straw or thatch. Such homes are often close together and set partially into the mountainsides. Ladders connect the lower dwellings to the higher ones.

NAMES

First names in Morocco are commonly Arabic and usually have a meaning.

POPULAR NAMES FOR GIRLS:
Amel (Hope)
Awatef (Feelings)
Kmar (Moon)
Latifa (Kindly)
Noura (Light)
Sana (Radiance)

POPULAR NAMES FOR BOYS:
Adil (Just)
Khaled (Eternal)
Mahdi (Rightly Guided)
Mourad (Desired)
Naji (Close Friend)

A group of Berbers have set up their tents near Fès. Moroccans who lead a nomadic lifestyle need homes that are easy to move.

Urban housing ranges from Western-style apartments and townhouses to the temporary shanties used by about 30 percent of all urban dwellers. Bidonvilles are slums named from the French *bidon*, meaning "tin can," and *ville*, meaning "city." Tin cans or metal oil drums, cut and flattened, are the main building material of the Moroccan slums.

Many urban poor live in large residences that have been subdivided into apartments. In some cases, an entire family may live in a single room. The government is building low-cost housing. But population growth and the large number of migrants from rural areas outstrip the government's ability to meet the needs for housing and services.

The government has improved water and sanitation systems for its citizens, but rural people still have far fewer services than people in cities. Only 80 percent of rural people have access to safe water compared to 98 percent of urban dwellers. Measuring access to sanitation (including sewage systems and garbage service), that number drops to 68 percent of rural people and 86 percent of urban people. Unclean water leads to the spread of communicable waterborne diseases.

Family Life and Women

The family is the basis of society in Morocco. Family loyalty and honor is very important to Moroccans. The family is a tight unit, with all

In Morocco's big cities, most people wear Western-style clothing, but many Moroccans still wear **traditional clothing.** Some women cover their head or face with a veil, in the Islamic tradition. Others don't veil, considering the tradition old-fashioned. Visit www.vgsbooks.com where you will find links to websites with more information about women in Morocco.

members helping one another out. The family is expected to provide emotional and economic support to all members. Many rural families, for instance, rely on income sent by relatives working in the cities. Extended families, including grand-parents, often live together. While this may be a crowded arrangement, Moroccans usually do not suffer from loneliness.

Morocco is a male-dominated society, and women have tradition-ally held a lower status than men. Under Morocco's 1957 *Mudawana*, or "family law," women did not have equal legal status with men. For instance, a man could divorce his wife simply by saying out loud in public that he divorced her. But a woman had to go to court to divorce her husband. Men could marry up to four wives, as allowed by Islam, without having the other wives' permission.

Nonetheless, women made great strides in Moroccan society since they won the right to vote and to run for political office in 1972. Women are active in all sectors of Moroccan life, working as politicians and royal advisers, businesspeople, Olympic athletes, journalists, and doctors.

Studies show that improved schooling for girls helps reduce poverty, as the girls grow up better able to participate in decision mak-ing. Education for women is also a major factor in improving children's health and nutrition, since women are the main caretakers of children in Morocco.

THE HUMAN DEVELOPMENT INDEX

The Human Development Index (HDI) measures human well-being, or the prospects of a person having a long, healthy life with education and a good standard of living. It is not a measure of happiness. The HDI is determined using key indicators such as life expectancy, literacy, and average income. The HDI value lies between 0 and 1. A value above 0.8 means high human development. A value below 0.5 reflects low human development. The UNDP (United Nations Development Programme) ranks the HDI of 177 countries.

HDI values and rankings:
Mauritania: value 0.454, ranking 154
Morocco: value 0.620, ranking 125
Algeria: value 0.704, ranking 108
Spain: value 0.918, ranking 19
United States: value 0.937, ranking 7

CULTURAL LIFE

Morocco's culture is a complex patchwork of traditions and innovations. *Ma'alem* means "master artisan" in Moroccan Arabic, and craftspeople in Morocco keep alive the traditional techniques of making useful and decorative items. But a new generation of artisans adds new ideas, such as weaving black-and-white plastic bags into baskets of striking designs. Writers, musicians, and architects also put together different styles, creating a vibrant blend of old and new, Arab and European. Whatever the different pieces, however, Morocco's culture is united by the Islamic faith.

○ Religion and Holidays

About 99 percent of Morocco's people are Muslims. Islam is the state religion, and the king is the country's religious and political leader. Islam is a monotheistic (one god) religion that shares roots with Judaism and Christianity. Muslims accept the prophet Muhammad as the last and greatest messenger of Allah, completing

the messages of Abraham, Moses, and Jesus. Muslims believe that Muhammad received the word of God through the angel Gabriel. These messages are recorded in the Quran. Muslims look to this holy book and the hadith, the written collection of Muhammad's sayings and deeds, for political and social guidance as well as spiritual inspiration.

Devout Muslims strive to fulfill Islam's basic duties, known as the Five Pillars of Islam. These five duties are making the statement of faith in God and the prophet Muhammad; praying five times daily; fasting during the holy month, Ramadan; giving to charity; and making a pilgrimage to the holy city of Mecca, Saudi Arabia, if possible.

Both Arabs and Berbers practice Islam in their daily lives. Berber groups may also include elements of folk religion in their beliefs. Many Berbers give special honor to holy figures of Islam, regarded as saints. This practice goes against strict Islamic tradition, which considers all Muslims to be equal.

There are also about seventy thousand Christians in Morocco and a Jewish community of about four thousand. In 1999 the government reopened a seventeenth-century synagogue (Jewish place of worship) in Fès.

Islamic holidays follow a lunar calendar. It is eleven days shorter than the solar year. Therefore, Islamic holy days do not always fall in the same season. The most important Islamic holy time is the month of Ramadan, the month when Allah called Muhammad to be his prophet. During Ramadan, observant Muslims do not drink anything, smoke, or eat between sunrise and sunset. The whole country slows down during Ramadan in the day. However, at night the cities are lively, and shops and cafés open. Ramadan ends with two days of celebration, called Eid al-Fitr. The other main Islamic holidays are Muharram 1, the first day of the Muslim year; Mouloud, the prophet Muhammad's birthday; and Eid el-Kebir (the Feast of the Sacrifice) remembering the prophet Abraham's obedience to God.

Morocco also has numerous regional festivals called *moussems* in honor of local Muslim saints. Orthodox Muslims frown on this practice, but Islam, like Christianity, is made up of many branches, and such religious festivals continue. A yearly festival in Salé, once a center of

Bicycles are lined up outside a **mosque in Marrakech.** The tower of the mosque is called the minaret. Calls to prayer are issued five times a day from loudspeakers in the minarets of each mosque.

piracy, honors the patron saint of Salé and of travelers. Festivities include a lantern parade and crowds of people dressed as pirates.

The nation observes many secular (nonreligious) public holidays. January 1 is New Year's Day. March 3 celebrates Muhammad VI becoming king. May 1 is Labor Day. November 6 remembers the Green March, and November 18 is Independence Day.

Local festivals revolve around agricultural activities. Annual festivals celebrate almond blossoms, honey, dates, horses, and more. In June Marrakech hosts the famous Festival of Folk Art and Music, a ten-day event attended by dancers, musicians, and other entertainers from around the country.

LUCKY HAND

Moroccan popular belief respects the power of the evil eye to bring bad luck. One way to ward it off is to show the open hand, palm facing out and fingers pointing upward. The five fingers also represent the five main duties of Islam. This "hand of Fatima" —named after the prophet Muhammad's daughter—is frequently painted on doors, depicted on stickers, or worn as jewelry.

▶ Literature and Media

Moroccan writers from the Moorish era of the tenth to the fourteenth centuries are among the world's great scholars and explorers. Ibn Battuta (1304–1377), sometimes called the Arab Marco Polo, traveled about 75,000 miles (120,700 km) over almost thirty years. The title of his account of his journey is *A Gift to Those Who Contemplate the Wonders of Cities and the Marvels of Travelling*. It is often simply called *Rihla*, or *Journey*. Some parts appear to be fictional, but nevertheless, the *Rihla* is the only account that exists of some parts of the world at that time.

Since the 1800s, many European writers have been fascinated with Morocco. British journalist Walter Harris wrote a classic piece of travel writing, *Morocco That Was*. He recorded his years in the late 1800s among sultans and warlords in an entertaining and readable style. One of the most famous French authors to write about Morocco is Antoine de Saint-Exupéry. An aviator as well as a writer, he was the airport chief in southern Morocco in the 1920s. He wrote his first novel, *Southern Mail*, there and later used desert images in his internationally beloved story *The Little Prince*.

Moroccan author Allal al-Fassi produced beautiful Arabic verse following World War I. But twentieth-century Moroccan authors wrote mostly in French. Driss Charibi and Ahmed Sefrioui are two of Morocco's most notable authors writing in French. Both writers examine conflicts around religion, progress, and foreign influences in their country. Charibi's first novel, *The Simple Past* (1954), made him one of the first Moroccan writers to achieve international fame.

American Paul Bowles (1910–1999) is the most famous author writing about Morocco in English. He spent most of his adult life in Tangier. His stories and essays explore North Africa with insight, humor, and sometimes violence. His novel *The Sheltering Sky* was made into a movie filmed in Morocco.

In 1987 Moroccan novelist, Tahar Ben Jelloun, won French literature's important Prix Goncourt for his novel, *The Sacred Night*. This novel tells the story of Zahra, a girl whose father was desperate for a son and raised her as a boy. At twenty Zahra enters the world for the first time as a woman. Ben Jelloun is also the author of *Islam Explained* (2004). It takes the form of a discussion between Ben Jelloun and his young daughter about what it means to be a Muslim in modern times. Ben Jelloun points out, for instance, that the Quran forbids terrorism.

Fatema Mernissi is a contemporary Moroccan writer who works for equal rights for women. For *Doing Daily Battle: Interviews with Moroccan Women* (1991), she interviewed women peasants, laborers, and servants. Leila Abouzeid is a noted Moroccan writer who writes in Arabic because she does not want to use the language of colonial rule. But her fiction attracts both Western and Middle Eastern readers. In her first novel, *Year of the Elephant*, the author presents common themes in Moroccan literature—the struggle against poverty and family conflict—from a woman's point of view.

THE POWER OF MEMORY

Swedish author Sven Lindqvist writes in his travel memoir *Desert Divers* (New York: Granta Books, 2002) of meeting a Saharan poet, Yara Mahjoub, in Morocco. Mahjoub is illiterate and cannot write even his name. However, as is common for people with a tradition of oral literature, he has a tremendous memory. He knows all his poems—thirty years' worth—by heart. He tells Lindqvist he can recite them "all night and all the next day and still have many unspoken."

New, worldwide communication technology has changed Morocco. The government can no longer tightly control public information as it traditionally has. Satellite TV—especially the all-Arab television Al Jazeera—cell phones, and the Internet have opened up communication. In large towns, Moroccans can pay to get online at Internet cafés.

Morocco publishes twenty-two daily newspapers, owned either by the government or privately. Freedom of the press is still officially limited. It is illegal to publish any attack on Islam, the monarchy, or Morocco's territorial holdings (to question the policy toward Western Sahara). Reporters have been jailed for offending the government. Low literacy levels limit Moroccans' access to information too.

Moroccan Cinema

Moroccan cinema began in 1897 with French filmmaker Louis Lumière's *Le Chevalier Marocain* (The Moroccan Knight) shot in the country. But the internationally famous World War II romance set in Morocco, *Casablanca* (1942), was filmed in Hollywood. In 1958 Mohammed Ousfour made the first Moroccan movie, *Le Fils Maudit* (The Damned Son), in French. Other Moroccan films followed.

Ouarzazate, Morocco, hosts the biggest movie studio in the world. Near the Sahara, the city is sometimes called the door to the desert. The varied scenery can appear as other places and times, and American moviegoers have often seen Morocco disguised as another country.

Ouarzazate, Morocco, is home to the largest movie studio in the world. Many well-known movies have been filmed there.

Director David Lean made *Lawrence of Arabia* there in 1962. The movie, with stunning scenes set in the Sahara, won seven Academy Awards. Director Ridley Scott used Morocco's various landscapes to make three films in the Ouarzazate area: *Gladiator* (2000), set in ancient Rome; *Black Hawk Down* (2001), set in Somalia; and *Kingdom of Heaven* (2005), set during the Crusades.

In the twenty-first century, Moroccan directors make many movies in their country. Director Nabil Ayouch's film *Ali Zaoua*, about a group of Casablanca street children, was made with local children. *Histoire d'une Rose* (Story of a Rose), directed by Abbylmajid R'chich, is about a woman trapped in an unhappy marriage. The Mediterranean Film Festival is held every year in Tètouan.

▶ The Arts

Ancient peoples of North Africa left behind works of art painted and carved into rock faces. Rock art sites in Morocco are in danger from illegal art collectors. Thieves have broken about 40 percent of the art off rock walls and smuggled it out of the country to sell.

Moroccan, or Moorish, architecture originated in contact with Arab and Spanish styles, beginning in the 700s. Artisans combined styles and created elaborate mosques, religious schools, and palaces. The buildings often have horseshoe-shaped arches, windows, and doorways.

City gates are common throughout Morocco. This gate to the medina, or old part of town, of Fès displays common features of **Moorish architecture.**

Geometric patterns of tile, marble, and wood decorate the walls and surfaces. Slender columns and outdoor courtyards are other hallmarks of Moorish style. Modern Moroccan cities reflect French influence, with Western-style apartment and office buildings.

Morocco influenced French arts too. Eugène Delacroix is considered the greatest French romantic painter. His visit to Morocco in 1832 provided subjects for many famous paintings. *Moroccan Journey: Travel Notebooks* are notebooks that Delacroix kept, that illustrated his journey to Morocco.

LIGHTING THE WAY

Ten thousand craftspeople worked on the Hassan II Mosque *(above)*, built on the seashore in Casablanca. It was completed in 1993, after five years' work. The world's third-largest religious monument, it cost millions of dollars to create. Powerful laser lights beam from the mosque in the direction of Mecca, Saudi Arabia, Islam's holy city. This is the direction all Muslims face when they pray.

This tannery is located in Fès. Morocco is famous for its leatherwork. These pits are full of dye to color the hides. To learn more about Moroccan arts, visit www.vgsbooks.com for links.

Moroccan crafts are world famous. Impressive leatherwork and jewelry, blue and white pottery, metal lanterns, and carpets are made in age-old ways. Painting traditionally was a purely decorative art in Morocco, and some of the finest work is found on the tile walls of mosques. By the early 1960s, however, Moroccan painters departed from the strict Islamic tradition that forbids artwork with human images. Although most of the nation's painters still create scenes from nature, many depict scenes of people and street life. In the twenty-first century, Moroccan author Fatema Mernissi works with Ruth V. Ward, an American photographer, on projects that mix images and words. Art exhibitions of their work about the roles of women are shown widely in Europe and the United States.

Music, Dance, and Sports

Like much of Morocco's culture, classical Moroccan music dates from the Moorish era. It also incorporates many Berber storytelling musical traditions. Students spend many years at music conservatories in Rabat and Marrakech. A music group might include a *darbuqa* (a funnel-shaped drum), a *tar* (a kind of tambourine), a *rebab* (a lutelike stringed instrument), and a *kemancha* (a violin that usually has only one string).

Popular Moroccan music features both Berber and Arab elements. Modern musicians fuse African, French, pop, and rock styles. *Griha* is the most widely played popular music, often combining the sounds of a viola and a two-stringed mandolin.

Dancing—an important part of harvest festivals, marriages, and funerals—usually features heavy rhythms provided by drums and tambourines. The ancient dance Westerners call belly dance is called *raks sharki* in Arabic, which means "Oriental dance." (The term *belly dance* was made up for the 1893 World's Fair in Chicago.) It is performed mostly for tourists, unlike Berber dances, which are still an authentic part of rural life. Different Berber groups present their particular dances in full ceremonial dress during the annual Marrakech Folk Festival.

Soccer, called football outside of the United States, is the favorite sport in Morocco and across North Africa. Morocco's national soccer team is nicknamed the Atlas Lions. In 1986 the team became the first African team to win a round of the international World Cup competition. Basketball and boxing are also popular in Morocco. Morocco sent seven boxers to the 2004 Olympic Games in Athens, Greece.

Morocco has produced several outstanding track-and-field stars. Moroccan runners won three medals at the 2004 Olympic Games. Hicham el Guerrouj, one of the greatest middle-distance runners of all times, won gold medals in the men's 1,500- and 5,000-meter races. Known as the King of the Mile, el Guerrouj set the world record for the mile in 1999. Hasna Benhassi is another middle-distance runner. She won a silver medal in the women's 800-meter race at the 2004 Olympics.

These two young Morrocan women play on a **soccer team in Rabat.**

Arabian horses, known for grace, endurance, and speed, have long been part of Moroccan history. At festivals throughout the country, men display their horse-riding skills in fantasias. These mock battle charges recall their ancestors' military skills on horseback.

Moroccan men and women often socialize separately. Men relax at coffee shops, while women usually gather with friends and family in the home. People often take a leisurely stroll at dusk, when the day cools off. Near the coasts, people like to go to the beach. Beach volleyball and surfing are popular with young people and tourists.

▶ Food

The scents and flavors of Moroccan cooking—including rose water, lemon, and cinnamon—delight the senses. Fragrant oils and spices such as cumin, ginger, or pepper flavor most meals. Cooking meat with fruit or nuts, such as chicken with apricots or lamb with almonds, typifies Moroccan cuisine.

Couscous, or steamed wheat, served with a spicy stew of meat and vegetables, is the national dish. *Tajine* is the name of both a flavorful stew and the clay pot the stew is cooked in. Moroccans eat lamb often, either roasted or as shish kebab (bite-sized bits of skewered lamb barbecued over coals). Meat pies take hours to prepare, as the fillings are layered in as many as fifty paper-thin sheets of pastry.

Homemade flat bread, dairy products such as yogurt, vegetables, and goat and mutton (sheep) meat are staples of the ordinary Moroccan diet.

Hot, sweet mint tea is a very common drink in Morocco.

MOROCCAN COCONUT FUDGE

This sweet is ideal to serve later in the evening, after a Moroccan dinner. Serve with hot mint tea, if you like. To make mint tea, add 3 tablespoons of dried mint leaves, 6 tea bags (oolong, or other black tea), and ½ cup sugar to a large teapot. Carefully fill teapot with boiling water. Steep tea for 5 minutes. Stir, strain into tea (or juice) glasses, and serve.

2 cups grated coconut (pack-
  aged or fresh)

¾ cup evaporated milk

2 cups sugar

1 tablespoon butter

2 tablespoons grated lemon rind
  (outer skin)

1. Combine coconut, evaporated milk, and sugar in a 2-quart saucepan. Heat over medium heat, and stir until boiling. Handle with care: boiling sugar is sticky and will burn skin.
2. Turn down heat and simmer, stirring frequently, until mixture reads 238°F on a candy thermometer, or until a soft ball is formed when a bit of candy is dropped into cold water.
3. Remove pan from heat. Add butter and lemon rind, and stir until butter melts.
4. Let candy cool to room temperature in the pan. Beat cool candy with a large spoon until thick and glossy.
5. Pour into a square 8 × 8-inch (20 × 20-cm) pan lined with wax paper. Chill, and cut into 1-inch squares.

Serves 8.

The most common vegetables are turnips, potatoes, and artichokes. By religious law, Muslims do not eat pork or drink alcohol.

The great variety of Moroccan fruit—oranges, grapes, and melons, for example—offers a cooling contrast to the highly seasoned main meals. A fig, some dates, or a handful of nuts are a common snack. Moroccans enjoy sweets, and desserts vary from cool custards to sticky honey pastries. Hot mint tea with lots of sugar is part of every meal, served in little glasses. Thick, dark, sweet Turkish coffee occasionally replaces tea. Moroccans drink fruit juices or water flavored with rose petals throughout the day.

Visit www.vgsbooks.com for links to websites with additional information about Morocco's culture and links to Moroccan recipes.

THE ECONOMY

Morocco's average income per person is $4,100, about average for developing countries and for North Africa. (In the language of economics, this is the GNI PPP per capita, or the gross national income, in purchasing power parity, per person. PPP converts a nation's currency into international dollars that calculate what the money could actually buy.) Developed countries, such as Spain, average $26,000 per person. More than 23 percent of Morocco's workforce is unemployed or underemployed (working at a level far below their training). Population growth also stresses the economy. About 300,000 new workers enter the nation's workforce every year, but only 20,000 new jobs are created.

The government is working to improve the economy with a number of reforms. It is in the process of selling 114 state-owned companies. Major sales have included the state's tobacco company, car company, and 35 percent of the telecommunication sector. Privatization (selling to private ownership) raises money for the

government and reduces its burden of running inefficient industries. Morocco's government also announced a plan called the 2020 Rural Development Strategy to improve standards of living and incomes in rural communities by 2020. This ambitious plan is investing in small-scale irrigation, rural roads, water supply, sanitation, health care, and schools.

Morocco is striving to improve its trade relationships with other countries. It is bidding for membership in the European Union (EU, an economic organization that removes barriers to movement of people, goods, and money among member nations). Europe is Morocco's main trade partner, but the EU does not consider Morocco's economy healthy and strong enough to let it into the union yet. In 2004 the United States and Morocco signed a fair trade agreement that removes almost all tariffs (taxes) on products the two countries trade. This agreement encourages new trade and investment.

Services and Tourism

The service sector of a country's economy provides services rather than producing goods. It includes jobs in government, health care, education, retail trade, banking, and tourism. Morocco's service sector accounts for 43 percent of Morocco's gross domestic product (GDP, the value of goods and services produced in a country in a year). Jobs in services employ 45 percent of Morocco's workers. The government is the largest employer, but this sector is bogged down with inefficiency.

Tourism is one of Morocco's main sources of foreign currency each year, though numbers dropped after the 2003 bombings in Casablanca. More than 2 million tourists spend about $2 billion in Morocco every year. Visitors come mostly from Europe, attracted to the sunny climate, ancient sights, and fabulous scenery. It is possible to ski down snowcapped mountains one day and ride a camel through sand dunes the next. Morocco's popular coastal resorts appeal to visitors looking for sun, sand, and sea. The country's souks, or open-air markets, offer a wealth of delights, including street musicians, acrobats, carpet merchants, leather goods, brightly colored silks, jewelers, and good things to eat. The nation's large network of hotels is well organized. Some of these accommodations are former palaces. The roads to main towns are good. Ferries from Spain allow people to bring their cars. Cruise ships also bring more than 200,000 passengers to Morocco's shores every year.

Industry, Mining, and Manufacturing

Industry, including mining and manufacturing, brings in 36 percent of Morocco's GDP. The industry sector employs 15 percent of the labor force.

Mining is Morocco's main industry. Phosphate mining is crucially important, accounting for 92 percent of mineral production. The phosphate rock in Morocco and in the disputed Western Sahara is estimated to total 75 percent of the world's reserves. The largest phosphate deposits in the world are mined in the country. It has a reserve of 110 billion tons (99.8 billion metric tons). Phosphate rock and phosphate products account for almost half of Morocco's total export earnings. The ports at both Casablanca and Safi receive heavy international traffic, because the world purchases over 40 percent of its phosphate from Morocco. The Moroccan government has invested heavily in processing plants to turn the raw mineral into finished fertilizers. Demand for phosphate has gone down because of concern, especially in North America, over the environmental hazards of phosphate-based fertilizers.

Sheep graze in front of a `phosphate mine.` Phosphate mining is Morocco's main industry.

Other mineral deposits—including coal, iron, and manganese—also exist in Morocco, but they are not as profitable as phosphate. The government encourages foreign investment in petroleum (crude oil) exploration, especially offshore in the Atlantic. So far, no major reserves have been discovered.

Casablanca is the manufacturing center of the country. Most manufacturing firms are small and produce goods for use in the nation, not exports. The chemical industry is the most profitable and accounts for about 33 percent of the nation's production. Textile and leather industries contribute about 15 percent of manufacturing output, while food processing supplies about 10 percent. Cement is made for the construction trades to build roads and housing.

Agriculture, Fishing, and Forestry

Agriculture, including livestock raising, forestry, and fishing, has long dominated Morocco's economy. Agriculture provides 21 percent of the country's GDP. About 40 percent of the population is employed in agriculture. Morocco's main agricultural products are barley, wheat, citrus fruits, wine, olives, and livestock. Morocco is a major food exporter, mostly of citrus fruits, especially oranges. The country also exports tomatoes, wine, and fresh and processed vegetables. Although once an exporter of wheat and maize (corn), Morocco imports wheat annually to feed its rapidly growing population. The country also consumes high levels of sugar, one of its main imports.

Donkeys are commonly used for plowing in Morocco. This sort of traditional farming method is not usually efficient enough to make a profit for the farmer.

Two reasons for the rise in cereal imports such as wheat are Morocco's growth in population and its drought-prone climate. Cereal products are more affected than other crops by variable moisture. If sufficient rain falls, the annual harvest produces enough to supply both local needs and export quotas. If rainfall levels are low, however, the government must import food to prevent widespread hunger. Increases in droughts since the early 1980s has led the government to improve citrus and wheat harvests. Government subsidies (payments) allow farmers to irrigate, plant higher quality seeds, and use more fertilizer. These improvements lead to larger and more reliable harvests.

Insufficient rainfall also severely affects the goats, sheep, and dairy cattle that graze on Morocco's farmland. Morocco has about 26 million livestock, including 17.3 million sheep.

Moroccans practice two distinct types of agriculture. A small number of wealthy Moroccan landowners—about 3 percent of the nation's farmers—employ modern machinery and techniques on large, irrigated farms. They mostly produce cash crops for export. Most landowners, however, run family farms smaller than 10 acres (4 hectares). These subsistence farmers raise food to feed their families, with little or none left to sell. They use traditional methods and tools, such as plows drawn by oxen, to work the nonirrigated, dry earth. Their success depends on rainfall to soften and water the soil. About 25 percent of the rural population lives below the poverty line (internationally set at less than two dollars a day).

In the isolated and poorly developed Er Rif Mountains, farmers cultivate cannabis, known in Morocco as kif. This illegal drug is prepared as marijuana or hashish. An estimated two-thirds of the rural population, mostly Berbers, depends on the sale of the crop. Most of it is smuggled to Europe by sea. The drug trade is estimated to earn $13 billion. But drug lords, largely Europeans, take most of the profits, not the farmers. The European Union has invested millions of dollars to help Morocco's government develop alternative forms of agriculture. Pilot projects are encouraging raising almond trees, keeping bees for honey, and livestock rearing.

Fishing is a major export industry in Morocco. The government has invested $151 million to improve the country's ports and fishing fleet. Powerful, refrigerated vessels replaced four hundred fishing boats. Sardines, tuna, mackerel, and anchovies are in plentiful supply in the Atlantic waters off the western coast of Morocco. The total haul of nearly 1 million tons (.9 metric tons) per year accounts for 9 percent of the country's total exports. Safi and Agadir are the main fishing ports, where the catch is packed and shipped to Casablanca to be processed. They are either canned or frozen for export or made into fertilizer or animal feed.

Morocco's most valuable trees are fir, cork oak, and cedar. Major products include timber, cork, panels, and crates. Pulp is also produced and sold within Morocco to manufacturers of paper and cardboard. Overgrazing and woodcutting by rural populations are also ongoing

Fishing boats line the harbor of Essaouira, Morocco.

6000 B.C.	Human hunter-gatherers lived on the Sahara's grasslands.
2000 B.C.	Berber farmers arrive in the area of present-day Morocco.
800s B.C.	Phoenicians build Carthage and spread across the Maghreb.
A.D. 200s	Romans controlling northern Morocco build the city of Volubilis.
429	The Vandals overrun the Maghreb and rule Morocco for the next century.
683	Arab Islamic armies come through the Taza Gap.
711	Tariq ibn Zayid and his army invade Vandal-held Spain. The resulting blend of Spanish and Moroccan cultures is called Moorish.
808	Moulay Idris II founds the city of Fès. The Idrisids (Idris family) firmly establish hereditary rule by sharifs.
859	Morocco's first university, the Islamic University of Fès, is founded.
1000s	Arab Bedouin nomads migrate to Morocco. The Almoravids gain control of Morocco and part of Spain.
1154	*The Pleasure of Excursions* by al-Idrisi is published, containing some of the world's first useful maps.
1248	Moors began building the Alhambra palace in Spain which is under Almohad control.
1276	The Merinids execute the last of the Almohads, outside Marrakech.
1300s	The Sufi branch of Islam spreads through North Africa, emphasizing personal spiritual practices.
1492	Christian crusaders defeat the last Moorish kingdoms in Spain. Jews are expelled from Spain.
1500s	Portuguese establish military bases as far south as Agadir and found the city of Casablanca.
1578	Ahmed al-Mansur comes to power. His soldiers reclaim Ceuta.
1600s	Sultan Moulay Ismail makes Meknès his capital. Muslims expelled from Spain.
1610	King Philip III of Spain expels Jews and Muslims from Spain. Many settle in Morocco.
1672	Alowite sultan Moulay Ismail begins his fifty-five-year rule. His descendants still rule Morocco.

1786   Sultan Sidi Muhammad signs business treaties with the United States.

1856   The opening of the Suez Canal in Egypt allows ships to sail from the Atlantic Ocean to the Indian Ocean.

1900   European powers have claimed vast sections of the African continent. More than ten thousand Europeans settle in Morocco.

1912   The Treaty of Fès makes Morocco a French protectorate. Moroccan children begin to attend French-style schools.

1926   French and Spanish forces crush the Er Rif rebellion.

1934   Sultan Muhammad V signs the Plan of Reforms submitted to him by Istiqlal (Freedom) Party nationalist leaders.

1943   Allied leaders at the Casablanca Conference lay plans to drive the Axis from the Mediterranean.

1956   Muhammad V and his new government begin ruling Independent Morocco.

1962   King Hassan II drafts Morocco's first constitution.

1972   Women win the right to vote. A second coup attempt against the king occurs.

1975   The Green March gathers 350,000 Moroccans, who march into Western Sahara.

1987   Tahar Ben Jelloun's novel *The Sacred Night* wins the important French literary prize, the Prix Goncourt.

1993   The Hassan II Mosque is completed in Casablanca.

1997   Ennakhil, a charity focusing on education, job training, and health, opens in Marrakech.

1999   Muhammad VI becomes king. A seventeenth-century Jewish synagogue reopens in Fès.

2002   King Muhammad VI marries Salma Bennani, a computer engineer.

2003   Bombings on May 16 in Casablanca kill more than forty people. Antiterrorism laws go into action.

2004   Changes in family law grant Moroccan women more equal rights with men. The United States declares Morocco a major ally. Morocco's soccer team wins second place in the African Nations Cup. Morocco runners win track medals at the Olympics.

2005   King Juan Carlos of Spain visits Morocco. Thousands of sub-Saharan Africans trying to escape poverty force entry into Ceuta.

COUNTRY NAME Kingdom of Morocco

AREA 172,413 square miles (446,550 sq. km)

MAIN LANDFORMS Coastal Lowlands, High Plateaus region, Interior Mountains (Anti-Atlas, Er Rif, Grand Atlas, Middle Atlas), Phosphates Plateau, Pre-Sahara region, Tangier Peninsula

HIGHEST POINT Mount Toubkal, 13,665 feet (4,165 m)

LOWEST POINT Sebkha Tah, 180 feet (55 m) below sea level

MAJOR RIVERS Bou Regreg, Moulouya, Oum er Rbia, Rheris, Sebou, Sous, Tensift, and Ziz

ANIMALS Barbary squirrels, cobras, eagles, fennecs, hawks, hyenas, jackals, jerboas, owls, scorpions, vipers, vultures

CAPITAL CITY Rabat

OTHER MAJOR CITIES Casablanca, Fès, Marrakech, Meknès, Tangier

OFFICIAL LANGUAGE Arabic

MONETARY UNITY Dirham (Dh). 100 centimes = 1 dirham.

CURRENCY

Banknotes (paper money) are issued in denominations of 20, 50, 100, and 200 dirhams. Coins come in denominations of 5, 10, 20, and 50 centimes. Centime coins are worth very little and are not much used. Coins also come in denominations of 1, 5, and 10 dirhams. The language on Moroccan money is in both French and Arabic. Both notes and coins carry the picture of King Hassan II on one side. It is considered wrong to deface, tear, or otherwise damage them, much as it would be considered wrong to damage a country's flag.

Currency   Fast Facts

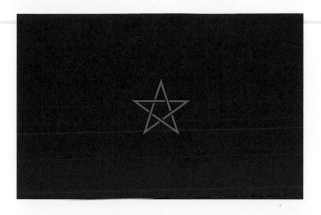

Morocco has used a red flag for centuries. The deep red color represents freedom and the descendants of the prophet Muhammad. Green is the color of Islam, and a green star is centered in the field of red. The star is called the Seal of Suleyman (or Solomon). Morocco introduced this flag in 1915 and officially adopted it at independence in 1956.

The music of the "Hymne Chérifien," written by Léo Morgan, has been Morocco's anthem since the country gained its independence in 1956. Ali Squalli Houssaini wrote new lyrics in 1970. An English translation follows below.

Hymne Chérifien

Fountain of Freedom, Source of Light
Where sovereignty and safety meet,
Safety and sovereignty, may you ever combine!
You have lived among nations with title sublime,
Filling each heart, sung by each tongue,
Your champion has risen and answered your call.
In my mouth and in my blood
Your breezes have stirred both light and fire.
Up! my brethren, strive for the highest.
We call to the world that we are here ready.
We salute as our emblem
God, Homeland, and King.

Visit www.vgsbooks.com for a link to a website where you can listen to Morocco's national anthem, "Hymne Chérifien."

LEILA ABOUZEID (b. 1950) Abouzeid is the first Moroccan woman writer whose literature was translated from Arabic into English. After studying at the Muhammad V University in Rabat and the University of Texas, she worked as a radio and TV reporter. Fellow of the World Press Institute in Saint Paul, Minnesota, Abouzeid left the press in 1992 to write fiction. Like many Moroccan writers, she uses the character of a storyteller in her stories. Her common themes explore the relations between men and women, old and new ways, and Western and Arab values. *The Last Chapter*, Abouzeid's latest book, is a partly autobiographical story about a young Moroccan woman. She lives in Rabat, Morocco.

HASNA BENHASSI (b. 1978) Benhassi is a middle-distance runner. At the 2004 Olympic Games in Athens, Greece, she finished second in the women's 800-meter race, winning a silver medal. She again won a silver medal in the 800-meter race at the World Championships in Athletics in August 2005.

TAHAR BEN JELLOUN (b. 1944) A novelist, essayist, journalist, and poet, Ben Jelloun was born in Fès and moved to France in 1971. His novels include *The Sacred Night*, *Corruption*, and *This Blinding Absence of Light*. In 1998 he wrote *Racism, as Explained to My Daughter* to answer questions about racism his ten-year-old daughter asked. It has been translated into fifteen languages. In 2004 *Islam Explained* followed the same format of a discussion between father and daughter.

HICHAM EL GUERROUJ (b. 1974) Born in Berkane, el Guerrouj is one of the greatest middle-distance runners of all times. Known as the King of the Mile, he is the world record holder for the 1,500 meters, the mile, and 2,000 meters. His sporting career is supplemented by his humanitarian work, and he is also a UNICEF Goodwill Ambassador. In 2002 the well-respected magazine *Track and Field News* chose him as best athlete of the year. In 2004 King Muhammad VI decorated el Guerrouj with the Cordon de Commandeur (Commander's Ribbon) award. In recent years, he competes in long-distance events.

ABU ABDULLAH MUHAMMAD IBN BATTUTA (1304–ca. 1377) Ibn Battuta was born into a Berber family in Tangier. He was an Islamic scholar, but he is best known for his travels. He traveled about 75,000 miles (120,700 km) over almost thirty years, more than traveler Marco Polo who lived near the same time. Ibn Battuta's journeys covered almost all the known Islamic world, extending also to present-day India, Sri Lanka, and China. At the request of the sultan of Morocco, several years after his return, ibn Battuta dictated an account of his journeys to a scholar, Ibn Juzayy. It is often simply referred to as the *Rihla*, or "Journey."

ABD AL-KRIM (ca. 1882–1963) Al-Krim, the son of an Islamic judge, was born in Ajdir into a Berber family. His full name was Muhammad Ibn Abd al-Karim Al-Khattab. He studied in Fès and Spain and worked for the Spanish government before he became the leader of a resistance movement against French and Spanish colonial rule in North Africa. In 1919 he began to unite the Berbers of Er Rif into an independent Republic of the Rif. In 1926 a combined French and Spanish army of 250,000 soldiers defeated the forces of al-Krim. He was sent into exile. In 1947 he was allowed to live in Egypt, where he oversaw the Liberation Committee for the Arab Maghreb. He died just after witnessing the independence of Algeria, the last Maghreb nation to achieve independence.

FATEMA MERNISSI (b. 1940) Mernissi was born in Fès and is a contemporary Moroccan teacher and writer. She studied political science in Paris and earned her doctorate at Brandeis University in Massachusetts. Mernissi writes about Islam and women's roles in it. Her topics include the wives of the prophet Muhammad, interviews with Moroccan women, and an autobiography. Mernissi also works with Ruth V. Ward, an American photographer, on projects mixing images and words. Art exhibitions of their work about the roles of women are shown widely in Europe and the United States. Mernissi teaches at the Muhammad V University and is a researcher at the University Institute for Scientific Research, both in Rabat.

KING MUHAMMAD VI (b. 1963) Born in Rabat, Muhammad was the first son of King Hassan II. Muhammad became king of Morocco in 1999, after the sudden death of his father. He supports social and political freedoms and economic development for his country. Still, Morocco remains a monarchy, and political realities reflect the king's personal views. Muhammad studied Morocco's position in international affairs and has his doctorate in law. In April 2002, in a three-day official wedding ceremony at the royal palace in Marrakech, he married computer engineer Salma Bennani. The publicity surrounding the marriage was a break with royal tradition in a country where details of kings' weddings were never discussed. In 2003 he and his wife had a son.

YOUSSEF SAFRI (b. 1977) is a Moroccan soccer player. He is best known for his passing skills. He was a key player with the Moroccan national team during the African Nations Cup of 2004, where Morocco came in second place.

FÈS The oldest of the royal cities, Fès became the spiritual and cultural heart of Morocco in the late 700s. Magnificent gates and walls, winding streets, and crumbling splendor fascinate visitors. The medina of Fès el-Bali (Old Fès) is one of the largest living medieval cities in the world. The old city contains bazaars, workshops, mosques, and the towering Medersa Bou Inania, a religious college built in 1350. Highly prized leather is made in Fès's tanneries.

MARRAKECH One of Morocco's most important cultural centers, Marrakech is famed for its markets and festivals. Visitors will find open-air food stalls, storytellers, snake charmers, magicians, and jugglers at the huge central square in the medina. Some of Morocco's best cuisine can be found in the restaurants here. Surrounded by date palm groves, the city is a good base for visiting nearby Grand Atlas Mountains and casbahs (walled fortresses).

RABAT The fourth of the royal cities, Rabat is a mix of history and modernization, and Morocco's French and Arab heritage. In the 1100s, the sultan used the casbah as a base for campaigns against the Spanish. The city's most famous landmarks date from this time. Rabat's modern atmosphere blends Islam and Europe in fairly equal proportions. European-style cafés coexist with mosques. The Archaeological Museum is one of the best museums in the country. Surfing on the Atlantic coast nearby is excellent.

SOUSS-MASSA NATIONAL PARK Located on the Atlantic coast, south of Agadir, this park's nature trails take visitors into a diverse landscape of cliffs, sand dunes, and forests. Bird-watchers can see a wide variety of birds here, including flamingos, eagles, ostriches, and the rare bald ibis, once a religious icon. Some rare mammals, such as the Egyptian mongoose, may also be glimpsed.

VOLUBILIS This long-abandoned city in the sand is the largest and best-preserved Roman ruin in Morocco. Its most impressive monuments, including temples, arches, and baths are from about A.D. 200. Unusually stunning mosaics (pictures made from tiny colored tiles) can still be seen in their original locations. Teams of French and Moroccan archaeologists continue to excavate this UNESCO world heritage site and find new discoveries. Camping sites are nearby.

Arabic: the official language of Morocco

casbah: (or kasbah) a citadel, a walled city or fortress in North Africa

couscous: a coarse grain, such as semolina, steamed and made into a spicy dish

desert: an area that receives less than 10 inches (25 cm) of rain a year and is therefore barren

desertification: the process of land turning into desert, caused by a combination of human and climate factors—drought, clearing land of plant life, and overuse of dry lands

fundamentalism: a movement within a larger group that wants strict observance of the group's basic (fundamental) principles and ideas

gross domestic product (GDP): the value of goods and services produced in a country in a year. Gross national product (GNP) adds in foreign income.

Islam: a religion founded in the seventh century A.D. based on the teachings of the prophet Muhammad. The holy book of Islam is the Quran.

literacy: the ability to read and write a basic sentence

Maghreb: Arabic word for northwestern Africa meaning "the land where the sun sets." Modern Maghreb nations are Morocco, Algeria, and Tunisia. Libya and Mauritania are sometimes included, and in 1989 the five nations formed the Arab Maghreb Union.

medina: Arabic for "town" or "city." It refers to a city's old central section.

mosque: an Islamic place of worship and prayer

Muslim: a follower of Islam. Almost all Moroccans are Muslims.

nationalist: a patriot, or person who feels supreme loyalty toward a nation and places the highest importance on promoting national culture and national interests

nomads: herders who move with their animals in search of pasture and water

oasis: a fertile place in the desert where underground water comes to the surface

purchasing power parity (PPP): PPP converts a country's currency into "international dollars" by calculating what money can buy in the country

Quran: the holy book of Islam. The prophet Muhammad dictated the book starting in A.D. 610. Muslims believe these scriptures come from God.

Sharia: Islamic holy law, the teachings and laws governing the lives of faithful Muslims, based on the Quran and the hadith, or sayings and actions of the prophet Muhammad

souk: a marketplace, traditionally with specific areas for different goods and trades, such as jewelry makers or carpets

Sunni: the major branch of Islam, including about 90 percent of all Muslims

Glossary

Selected Bibliography

BBC News. 2005.
http://www.bbc.co.uk (October 2005).
The World Edition of the BBC (British Broadcasting Corporation) News is updated throughout the day, every day. The BBC is a source for comprehensive news coverage about Morocco and also provides a country profile.

Central Intelligence Agency (CIA). "Morocco." *The World Factbook.* **April 2005.**
http://www.odci.gov/cia/publications/factbook/geos/__??__html (June 2005).
This CIA website provides facts and figures on Morocco's geography, people, government, economy, communications, transportation, military, and more.

Coulson, David. "Ancient Art of the Sahara." *National Geographic,* **June 1999, 98–120.**
Moroccan and other North African rock art sites have survived the elements for thousands of years. In modern times, thieves remove and tourists damage them. This article tells the story and documents the paintings and carvings in beautiful photographs.

Cutter, Charles H. *Africa 2004.* **Harpers Ferry, WV: Stryker-Post, 2004.**
The article on Morocco in this annual volume of the World Today series provides a moderately detailed look at the recent culture, politics, and economics of the country.

Diagram Group. *History of North Africa.* **New York: Facts on File, 2003.**
Part of the Peoples of Africa series, this book clearly presents historical information essential to understanding North Africa's recent political history. Glossary, illustrations, and maps are included.

———. *Peoples of North Africa.* **New York: Facts on File, 1997.**
This book is part of the Peoples of Africa series. It presents the different cultures and traditions of the major ethnic groups of North Africa, including the Berbers and Arabs of Morocco.

Economist. 2005.
http://www.economist.com (October 2005).
A weekly British magazine available online or in print, the *Economist* provides in-depth coverage of international news, including Morocco's political and economic news. The *Economist* also offers country profiles with relevant articles as well as some statistics at http://www.economist.com/countries.

Fletcher, Matt, J. Connolly, F. L. Gordon, and D. Talbot. *Morocco.* **Footscray, AU: Lonely Planet, 2001.**
Lonely Planet guidebooks are created for those who want to explore and understand the world. This guide includes a wealth of information from historical facts to where to go surfing in Morocco. Includes maps, photos, and all sorts of useful information. Lonely Planet also has an online site *Destination Morocco* at http://www.lonelyplanet.com/worldguide/destinations/africa/ morocco.

Harris, Walter. *Morocco That Was.* **London: Eland Books, 1921.**
This is a firsthand report on Morocco from the late 1800s and early 1900s by a reporter for the *Times* of London. Harris lived through the reign of three sultans and writes interestingly about Moroccan court life.

Holliday, Jane. *Morocco.* **London: A&C Black, 2002.**
This Blue Guide travel book offers good practical information about planning a trip to Morocco as well as ample background information on the country.

Lindqvist, Sven. *Desert Divers.* **New York: Granta Books, 2002.**
Part travel book, part personal reflection, part history, this book is an imaginative look at foreigners' love affair with the desert and their exploitation of it. Lindqvist writes of historical travelers and his own travels in the Maghreb, including meeting Moroccan poet Yara Mahjoub.

McGuinness, Justin. *Morocco Handbook.* **Bath, UK: Footprint Handbooks, 2001.**
This is a more in-depth guidebook to Morocco than most, providing detailed maps, history, and cultural information, including recipes.

The Middle East and North Africa 2005. **London: Europa Publications, 2005.**
The long section on Morocco in this annual publication covers the country's recent history, geography, and culture, as well as providing a detailed look at the economy and government of the country. Statistics are also included.

Population Reference Bureau. **2005.**
http://www.prb.org (October 2005)
PRB's annual statistics provide in depth demographics on Morocco's population, including birth and death rates, infant mortality rates, and other statistics. Special articles cover environmental and health issues.

Rogerson, Barnaby. *A Traveller's History of North Africa.* **Brooklyn: Interlink Books, 1998.**
Covering Morocco, Tunisia, Libya, and Algeria—countries with shared as well as individual history—this book considers North Africa to be "an island surrounded by three seas, the Mediterranean, the Atlantic, and to the south by the sand seas of the Sahara." The complex cultural background of the region is woven with a colorful cast of characters in this very readable history. Maps, a timeline, list of rulers, and illustrations accompany the text.

Smith, Craig S. "Hungry Goats Atop a Tree, Doing Their Bit for Epicures." *New York Times*, **October 27, 2005.**
This article looks at cooperatives working with local people to produce oil from Morocco's unique argan trees. Goats eat the argan fruit and spit out or excrete the pits. These are gathered to make oil for cooking or cosmetics.

U.S. Department of State, Bureau of Near Eastern Affairs. *Background Note: Morocco.* **2005.**
http://www.state.gov/r/pa/ei/bgn/5431.htm (June 2005).
The background notes of the U.S. State Department supplies a profile of Morocco's people, history, government, political conditions, economy, and more.

Weatherby, Joseph N. *The Middle East and North Africa: A Political Primer.* **New York: Longman, 2002.**
An overview of the forces that shape the part of the world that includes Morroco. It includes land and water issues, a history of colonialism, and more.

Abouzeid, Leila. *The Director and Other Stories from Morocco.* **Austin: University of Texas Press, 2006.**

Abouzeid is one of Morocco's most well-known modern authors. This collection of her short stories deals with traditional and modern issues in Morocco, such as the relations between parents and children and between men and women.

Ayoub, Abderrahman, et al. *Umm El Madayan: An Islamic City through the Ages.* **Boston: Houghton Mifflin, 1994.**

Umm El Madayan, or the Mother of Cities, is a fictional city representing any of many cities on Morocco's Mediterranean coast. Finely detailed pen drawings by Francesco Corni wonderfully illustrate the historical, architectural, and cultural development of the city as it evolves from a hunting-gathering site to a Phoenician colony to a Roman, then Arab city and so on.

Ben Jelloun, Tahar. *Islam Explained.* **Toronto: University of Toronto Press, 2004.**

This book for young readers is a clear introduction to the history, politics, and main beliefs of Islam. It is presented in question-and-answer format. The book also defines words often heard in the news, such as *terrorist*, *crusade*, *jihad*, and *fundamentalist*.

The Best of Morocco
http://www.morocco-travel.com
All the information you need to plan a trip to Morocco, including maps, images of the country, and information about destinations, transportation, and prices.

Blauer, Ettagale, and Jason Lauré. *Morocco.* **New York: Children's Press, 1999.**

Part of the Enchantment of the World series, this book for younger readers has lots of photos, facts and figures, and information about Morocco's history, culture, plants, animals, people, and land.

Fernea, Elizabeth Warnock, and Basima Bezirgan. *Middle Eastern Muslim Women Speak.* **Austin: University of Texas Press, 1977.**

This anthology draws from many sources and countries and provides an excellent overview of real lives of women in the Near and Middle East, including Morocco.

Freud, Esther. *Hideous Kinky.* **New York: Harper, 1992.**

In this novel, based partly on her own childhood, Freud tells the story of Julia, a hippie mother traveling from Tangier to Marrakech with her young daughters, Lucia and Bea, in the 1960s. The story is told through the eyes of five-year-old Lucia. The title reflects a word game using the phrase *hideous kinky*. This book was made into a movie starring Kate Winslet in 1998.

Gordon, Matthew. *Islam.* **Rev. ed. New York: Facts of File, 2001.**

This book is part of the World Religions series. It provides an overview of Islam, Morocco's official religion, discussing the religion's history, basic beliefs, and the modern Islamic world. Illustrations accompany the text.

Moroccan National Tourist Office
http://www.tourism-in-morocco.com
This site has information on traveling to Morocco.

Further Reading and Websites

"Morocco." *University of Pennsylvania, African Studies Center.*
http://www.sas.upenn.edu/African_Studies/Country_Specific/Morocco.html
The African Studies Center offers many links to online resources to find information about Morocco, concerning everything from comic books to human rights abuses. The mission statement of the center says it is a "center where researchers, students and cultural and business entities come to gain knowledge of contemporary and historical Africa."

Morocco Times
http://www.moroccotimes.com
This site of Morocco's English-language paper is updated online daily.

Oufkir, Malika, and Michéle Fitoussi. *Stolen Lives: Twenty Years in a Desert Jail.* **Translated by Ros Schwartz. New York: Hyperion, 2001.**
Malika Oufkir was born in 1953 and grew up in the royal palace of King Hassan. Her father, General Oufkir, was executed after an attempted coup against the king in 1972. The six Oufkir children and their mother were arrested and kept in a desert jail until they managed to dig a tunnel with their hands and escape. An Oprah Winfrey's book club selection, this book is a story of courage and hope. The author also writes with an insider's perspective of royal Moroccan women's lives.

Tayler, Jeffrey. *Glory in a Camel's Eye: Trekking through the Moroccan Sahara.* **Boston: Houghton Mifflin, 2003.**
Tayler spent two years in the Peace Corps in Marrakech before traveling across the Moroccan Sahara with camels and guides. They follow an ancient caravan route through the Draa Valley, a wilderness of sand and rock. Tayler, a journalist, writes of Morocco's historical and modern culture and politics, as well as recording the sandstorms, drought, date palms, camels, and descendants of the prophet Muhammad he encounters. The journey ends at the *bahr-al-zulumat*, meaning the "Sea of Darkness," the old Arabic name for the Atlantic Ocean.

Thompson, Craig. *Carnet de Voyage: Travel Journal Volume One.* **Marietta, GA: Top Shelf Productions, 2004.**
This is the travel diary drawn by cartoonist Craig Thompson while traveling through Morocco and Europe in spring 2004. Sketches and journal entries document Thompson's adventures and thoughts while he researched his next graphic novel.

vgsbooks.com
http://www.vgsbooks.com
Visit vgsbooks.com, the home page of the Visual Geography Series®, which is updated regularly. You can get linked to all sorts of useful online information, including geographical, historical, demographic, cultural, and economic websites. The vgsbooks.com site is a great resource for late-breaking news and statistics.

Winget, Mary, and Habib Chalbi. *Cooking the North African Way.* **Minneapolis: Lerner Publications Company, 2004.**
The cuisines of North Africa—Morocco, Algeria, Tunisia, Libya, and Egypt—are featured in this cultural cookbook. Besides offering a sampling of recipes, this book looks at the different peoples and customs.

Captions for photos appearing on cover and chapter openers:

Cover: The casbah of Ait Benhaddou is a UNESCO world heritage site. It has been featured in many movies including *Lawrence of Arabia* (1962).

pp. 4–5 The town of Essaouira is located on the coast of central Morocco.

pp. 8–9 The snowcapped Atlas Mountains rise behind a Berber village in east-central Morocco.

pp. 20–21 Roman ruins are found at Volubilis near the city of Meknès.

pp. 38–39 Schoolchildren in Marrakech smile for a photo on their way home from school.

pp. 46–47 Moroccan pottery has distinct designs that come from the influence of Islamic art.

pp. 58–59 Moroccans sell handmade crafts from jewelry to rugs at outdoor markets called souks. This souk is in Marrakech.

Photo Acknowledgments
The images in this book are used with permission of: © Simon Reddy/Art Directors, pp. 4–5; © XNR Productions, pp. 6, 11; © M. Jelliffe/Art Directors, pp. 8–9; © John Elk III, pp. 10, 58–59; © Robert Fried Photography/ www.robertfriedphotography.com, pp. 13, 14, 24, 38–39, 44–45, 48, 52, 53, 54–55, 56; © Yoshio Tomii/SuperStock, p. 17; © A. A. M. Van der Heyden/ Independent Picture Service, p. 18; © Helen Rogers/Art Directors, pp. 20–21, 40; © North Wind Picture Archives, p. 23; Illustrated London News, p. 31; © Nogues Alain/CORBIS SYGMA, p. 33; © Moroccan Government/ZUMA Press, p. 35; © Art Directors, p. 43; © China/SuperStock, pp. 46–47; © Jean-Leo Dugast/Panos Pictures, p. 49; © age fotostock/SuperStock, pp. 51, 63; © Eric Miller/Panos Pictures, p. 55; © Nik Wheeler/CORBIS, p. 61; © M. Good/Art Directors, p. 62; Audrius Tomonis–www.banknotes.com, p. 68.

Cover photo: © Sandro Vannini/CORBIS. Back cover photo: NASA.